THEY CHANGED THE GAME

— *Sports Pioneers of the Twentieth Century* —

KEN RAPPOPORT *and* BARRY WILNER

Andrews McMeel
Publishing

Kansas City

THEY CHANGED THE GAME

Copyright © 1999 Lionheart Books, LTD.

Printed in Canada. No part of this book may be used or reproduced in any manner
whatsoever without written permission except in the case of reprints in the context of reviews.
For information, write Andrews McMeel Publishing, an Andrews McMeel Universal company,
4520 Main Street, Kansas City, Missouri 64111.

www.andrewsmcmeel.com

99 00 01 02 TRC 10 9 8 7 6 5 4 3 2 1

Library of Congress Cataloging-in-Publication Data on File

Produced by Lionheart Books, Ltd.
Atlanta, Georgia 30341

Design: Jill Dible
Edited by: Gina Webb

TABLE OF CONTENTS

Preface v

Introduction – Jim McKay 1

THE BABE AND THE TWO BOPPERS – Babe Ruth, Mark McGwire, and Sammy Sosa 4

THE FIRST ONE – Jackie Robinson 14

THE GREATEST – Muhammad Ali 23

THE BIRDMAN, THE SHOWMAN AND THE MAN – Larry Bird, Magic Johnson, and Michael Jordan 35

THE OTHER BABE – Babe Didrikson Zaharias 46

QUEEN OF THE TRACK – Jackie Joyner-Kersee 51

BILLIE JEAN – Billie Jean King 55

THE GREATEST ONE – Wayne Gretzky 59

THE BLACK PEARL – Pele 63

ONE GOLDEN MOMENT – Jim Thorpe 67

PIVOTAL PLAYERS – George Mikan, Wilt Chamberlain, and Bobby Orr 72

COMMISSIONER PETE AND BROADWAY JOE – Pete Rozelle and Joe Namath 78

FLOOD TIDE – Curt Flood 85

KING OF THE ROAD – Richard Petty 89

INSPIRATION MAN – Knute Rockne 97

THE COWBOY AND THE KING – Tex Rickard and Don King 102

CALIFORNIA, THERE HE GOES – Walter O'Malley 109

THE SPRINTER AND THE MILER – Jesse Owens and Roger Bannister 113

THE TENNIS ACE – Arthur Ashe 119

CLARKSVILLE COMET – Wilma Rudolph 123

THE MOUTH THAT ROARED – Howard Cosell 127

THE VISIONARY – Roone Arledge 131

THE GALLOPING GHOST, THE SLINGER AND THE PROFESSOR – Red Grange, Sammy Baugh, and Sid Luckman . . 135

ARNIE, JACK AND TIGER – Arnold Palmer, Jack Nicklaus, and Tiger Woods 143

Acknowledgments 153

Photo credits 154

Special thanks to Joe Browne, Bob Greene, John Griffin and Tony Signore for their help on this project. And this project wouldn't have come to fruition without the understanding and encouragement of my wife Helene and children Nicole, Jamie, Tricia and Evan.

BARRY WILNER

For Bernice, my soulmate for all seasons.

KEN RAPPOPORT

PREFACE

Picking a "top" sports list of any kind has become trendy in America as the twentieth century comes to a close. We think this collection of 37 people is unique, because it deals not only with special athletes and personalities, but those who stretched the boundaries of their sports, and in some cases, the boundaries of our society.

From Babe Ruth to Babe Didrikson Zaharias, the stories all reflect some kind of change: a social change, as in the case of Jackie Robinson; a constitutional change, as in the case of Curt Flood; and a change in the way a game or a position is played, as in the case of Bobby Orr and Magic Johnson.

There were greats that you might expect to find in this book — Joe DiMaggio, Jim Brown, Kareem Abdul-Jabbar, Joe Montana, Gordie Howe, Sugar Ray Robinson and Bill Tilden to name just a few. But while these extraordinary athletes defined their places in their particular sports, they did not redefine how their sport was played or perceived. Nor was society changed in any way by their presence.

The people who were selected for *They Changed The Game* were special because of the kind of impact their presence created.

When Flood challenged baseball's reserve clause, it was an unpopular stand at the time. He wasn't the only one to create a public furor. Muhammad Ali, a boxing braggart, and Walter O'Malley, the "most hated man in Brooklyn," also stirred up negative emotions. Nor can you forget "The Mouth That Roared," Howard Cosell.

We also experienced exhilaration when our champions came through for us, and for their sports.

Ruth, Mark McGwire and Sammy Sosa carried baseball a long way with the long ball, while Wayne Gretzky and Pele blazed new trails for hockey and soccer, respectively, in North America.

Would the NBA have made it as big without Michael, Magic and Bird? Would football have become as popular without Rockne and the forward pass? Or would golf have the following it has today without Arnie and Jack, and a "Tiger" to bring it into a new millennium?

These twentieth-century pioneers raised the standards of their sports and built a path for others to follow. Because of their presence, the sports world entered a new world.

We can only imagine what the next 100 years will bring in terms of breakthroughs and great athletic achievements.

On to the new century.

The Authors

INTRODUCTION

by Jim McKay

One test of enduring fame in sports is the ability of the average sports fan to identify the person by a single name, or nickname.

Try these: The Babe, Ali, Jackie, Knute, Michael, Pele, Wilt, Arnie, Jack, Tiger, the Babe (female), Billie Jean, Jesse, King Richard, Wonderful Wilma, Roone.

If you are worth your weight in hot dogs, peanuts and beer, you got them all—and you will find them all in this book They span the years from World War I to Kosovo, from the time when all baseball games were played in broad daylight to an era when even World Series games end long after kids should be in bed, from hickory-shafted golf clubs to space-age titanium drivers, from all-white sports icons to the Rainbow Coalition of today's stars.

In my lifetime, I've been fortunate enough to have met the Babe (male) in person, and to still be active in my job as the heroes of the new millennium begin to appear.

I was ten years old when I met Babe Ruth in the early 1930s. My best friend's father knew the great man and took us to the Bellevue Stratford Hotel in Philadelphia for the biggest event of my first decade on earth. In the lobby we saw Lou Gehrig, reading the headline "Gehrig hits four against A's" in the *Philadelphia Inquirer*—four home runs that is, against my poor, down-trodden Philadelphia A's, the day before. No one has hit more in a game since then.

My friend's dad also knew Gehrig, and asked him if the Babe had appeared yet that morning.

"No," the Iron Man said with a smile. "He's in his room. Call him on the house phone."

A few minutes later, we stood outside the door leading to God. Tommy and I literally held our breath as the knob turned, the door opened and a barrel-chested man in a silk dressing robe stood before us.

"Hiya, kids," he said. "Come on in."

Our meeting was brief, just a couple of minutes, an autographed baseball for each of us, tickets for that day's game, and a pat on the back. But I had stored away a memory that is as crystal-clear in my mind today as it was then.

Even now, I am loath to read about my hero's drinking bouts, his gluttonous appetite or his womanizing. The expression "role model" didn't come into vogue until long years later, but the Babe was the original role model, an outsized hero who changed the status of the athlete forevermore.

If the hero-athlete has any significance in our society, it lies in his symbolic acts of grace and courage, not in his falls from grace. Save the mistakes for the police blotter—just tell me about excellence in the sports pages.

Tell me about Mark McGwire going to Roger Maris' family after his historic home run, picking up his own little boy, hugging his friendly rival, Sammy Sosa.

Remind me of the simple Native American nobility of Jim Thorpe, and of his stolid acceptance when they stole his Olympic medals from him, leaving the crusade for their recovery to his descendants.

Sing the praises of Jackie Robinson, enduring the disgusting curses of opposing teams as he opened baseball to the talents of the great African-American players.

Let the police reporter cover the drug abuse stories, or the bar fights, but don't let me forget that there was once a Red Grange, galloping across the football fields of the '20s with the grace of an elusive ghost. Or a Knute Rockne, urging his men to "win one for The Gipper."

Or a young English physician breaking the supposedly unassailable barrier of the four-minute mile, then returning to the practice of medicine.

Babe Zaharias, explaining her ability to hit man-sized tee shots by saying, "Honey. I just loosen up my girdle and let go," and later giving a lesson in courage by her uncomplaining fight against cancer.

These are the stories I want to hear, like a child asking for a favorite bedtime story again and again. I want my grandchildren to hear them, too. They'll hear plenty too much of the bad stuff in due time.

Unrealistic? Sure, but what is accomplished by puncturing a colorful balloon?

If it is a teacher who beats up children, a doctor who peddles drugs on the side, or an airline pilot who secretly has a few vodkas before taking 200 people into the sky, of course the tawdry side of their character is important to us.

But athletes don't harm us by their misdeeds. They can inspire us by their heroic side. It isn't important whether an anonymous little boy did or did not say to Shoeless Joe Jackson of the disgraced Chicago White Sox team that threw the World Series, "Say it ain't so, Joe." It IS important that youngsters often feel that way. They want to emulate that figure on the pedestal, not knock it to pieces.

I suppose this book appeals to me because it embodies much of what I have tried to communicate in my own career. "The thrill of victory and the agony of defeat—the human drama of athletic competition," is not just a slogan. It has been the philosophy of "ABC's Wide World of Sports" with which I am most associated since its inception, since our first program on April 29, 1961.

I have had the opportunity to watch many of this book's heroes and heroines as they changed their games, and often changed themselves in the process.

I first met Muhammad Ali when he won the light-heavyweight gold medal in the Olympics. I interviewed him at the New York airport as he came off the plane from that triumph. He was very young, not particularly brash, and offered no poems. But there was a presence about him that made you think there was much more to come. Through the years, we watched him change his game and restore some of the glory to boxing, if only temporarily.

We have had the opportunity to watch Arnold make golf an aggressive athletic endeavor, Nicklaus accomplish feats never dreamed of, and Tiger open the game to every kid who can get a couple of old clubs and make his way to a public golf course.

While I was at CBS in the '50s, I interviewed the young Dr. Roger Bannister, a few days after he had run the world's first sub-four-minute mile. On the same day, he cancelled an appearance on an American panel show when he found that its sponsor was a cigarette manufacturer. Yes, there was a time when cigarettes were allowed to pollute the airwaves as well as the lungs, but Dr. Bannister (a cardiologist) wouldn't be a part of it, long before the rest of us came to our senses.

Just a few months before his death, I asked Arthur Ashe to come to Baltimore and speak to the student body of Loyola College, my alma mater. He spoke to all the young people, male and female, but had some special words for the athletes, reminding them that there was more for them to learn in the classroom than there was on the athletic field, that an athletic scholarship was not a prize, but an opportunity; not an end, but a means.

I also knew Jesse Owens in the late autumn of his life, when he worked with me as an analyst on track and field telecasts. To the end, he was just as straight and tall, as dignified and as courageous as he was on the day he humiliated Hitler with the simple message of his talent.

We started covering stock car racing in the early '60s, when its appeal was still confined to the South. But we turned the spotlight on a handsome, smiling young driver from a place called Level Cross, and Richard Petty proceeded to make his smile, his big cowboy hat, his sunglasses and his great ability a matter of national interest.

Howard Cosell and Roone Arledge? To me, the most important thing about Howard was not his penchant for four-syllable words or his bombastic manner, but the fact that what you saw was what you got, that this was no contrived Howard Cosell "persona." Howard on screen was exactly as he was in private life.

Roone, of course, changed the way sport is covered forevermore (later, he did the same with news). He ushered in new camera angles—cameras dangling from cranes, cameras under water, cameras on the tips of skis—but his philosophy was more important. He was looking for the people embodied in the title of this book—people who were changing the game—and we found them.

The search goes on, because sports are in for much more change in the new millennium. What will the changes be? I don't know, but that is what intrigues me and keeps me fascinated after 50 years in the business.

Not only the changes to come, but the men and women who will have great ability and something more, the mind-set that Robert F. Kennedy suggested when he said, "Some people see what is, and say 'Why?'

Others see what might be and say, 'Why not?' "

THE BABE AND
THE TWO BOPPERS

Babe Ruth, Mark McGwire and Sammy Sosa

In the midst of the spectacular 1998 baseball season, a story surfaced that reflected, as much as anything that summer, the pulse and the heartbeat of an entire nation.

Three policemen in New England had been wounded in a shootout and rushed to a hospital for emergency surgery. Waking up after the operation, and still groggy, one of the officers supposedly asked:

"Did he hit one?"

He wasn't referring to the shootout; he was talking about either Mark McGwire or Sammy Sosa. So was everyone else in the country during the greatest home-run race in the history of baseball.

Sosa and McGwire's down-to-the wire battle was the perfect antidote for the national pastime, which had been on the disabled list for a couple of years following the strike in 1994 and the cancellation of the World Series.

Just when you thought it wasn't "cool" to go back to a baseball game, along came a pair of cool guys wearing the white hats and riding over the hill to save the sport.

Not unlike another time in America when a different Great Home Run Race also created national interest in every city in America from Austin to Boston…

The individual race between Babe Ruth and Lou Gehrig heated up the summer of 1927 and was just as important to baseball's best interests as the McGwire-Sosa home run derby some 70 years later.

Actually, Ruth had been doing his own thing a few years earlier to help revive baseball after the notorious "Black Sox" scandal of 1920. If Yankee Stadium was the House That Ruth Built, then baseball was the Sport That Ruth Rebuilt.

Born in 1895, George Herman

If Yankee Stadium was the House That Ruth Built, then baseball was the Sport That Ruth Rebuilt.

"All I wanted was to play. I didn't much care when."

Ruth grew up on the rough streets of Baltimore at the turn of the century. Unsupervised, he ran wild at an early age and was soon more than his saloon-keeper parents could handle. At age seven, he was declared incorrigible by his father and turned over to a Catholic home for boys. Not a model student, the dark-haired Ruth would sometimes cut classes to go fishing. But he was always there for sports, and he especially loved baseball. "All I wanted was to play. I didn't much care where." Ruth was a talent. Soon enough, he was trying out for the minor-league Baltimore Orioles.

The Sultan of Swat. The King of Clout. The Bambino.

These nicknames weren't yet a part of the American lexicon, but the "Babe" was about to be christened. The Orioles' manager, Jack Dunn, was so impressed with Ruth's arm, he quickly signed the 18-year-old to a professional contract and became his legal guardian. Young and raw, the newest recruit arrived at the Orioles' clubhouse in 1914. A veteran spied the new kid on the block and shouted, "Well, here's Jack's newest babe, now." And so "Babe" Ruth was born.

He might have been the new kid on the block but he played like a veteran. A player who would terrorize pitchers for years to come as the most feared hitter of his time, Ruth first made his mark as a pitcher. Midway through the 1914 season, the cash-strapped Orioles sold Ruth to the Boston Red Sox. The Red Sox had landed a winner.

"With the Red Sox, I really began to learn a little baseball," Ruth said. "I didn't think much of becoming a slugger. I like to hit, but it was pitching that took my time in Boston."

How good was Ruth as a pitcher? Only one of the best left-handers in the game, he could easily have been a shoo-in for the Hall of Fame. But as a pitcher, he would never have had the impact he did on the game. Ruth was too good a hitter not to use on an everyday basis.

So when he wasn't pitching, Ruth was playing the outfield, and in the summer of 1919 he crashed a record 29 home runs with the Red Sox.

And then, the baseball world itself came crashing down when eight Chicago White Sox players, accused of taking bribes from gamblers to throw the World Series went on trial—and so did the sport itself.

The American people always loved their heroes. When the scandal broke, it broke the hearts of millions—after all, baseball had always represented what was decent and fair about the U.S.A. Baseball was peanuts and hotdogs and the

American way of life. Fans were hurt and disillusioned. They felt betrayed.

The country needed a ninth-inning rally, and stepping up to the plate was Babe Ruth: wearing a New York Yankees uniform. The Red Sox had needed the money and the Yankees, the second-class citizen in New York behind the Giants, needed a box-office draw.

Ruth was the ticket.

When the Babe grabbed a bat, he grabbed hold of the fans' imagination. While other players hit home runs, none hit them like he did. They went out faster, traveled farther and created more excitement than any other player's homers. Ruth's home runs, according to Hall of Fame pitcher Walter Johnson, made the fans "so crazy with excitement that they were ready to tear up the stands."

An American original with a huge appetite for life, the gregarious, theatrical Ruth did everything in a big way. When he joined the Yankees, he predicted he would hit 50 home runs—outrageous, because no team in either league had hit 50 in 1919. He did better. He hit 54.

This No. 1 goodwill ambassador for baseball not only created a whole new style of play with the long ball, he also brought a sense of theater to the game.

Who can forget Ruth pointing to center field in the 1932 World Series, signaling that he was going to hit a home run, then actually hitting one in that very same spot?

Or the home run he delivered in the 1926 World Series for little Johnny Sylvester, the sick boy in the hospital, on the same day Sylvester asked for it?

When the Babe grabbed a bat, he grabbed hold of the fans' imagination. While other players hit home runs, none hit them like he did.

Apocryphal or not, the stories grew with Ruth's legend.

As fans flocked to see baseball's beloved hero, the Black Sox scandal faded into the background. And at the same time he was giving the game back to the American people, Ruth gave the Yankees everything they could hope for—not just home runs, but their own home. Their box-office success soared with Ruth on the team, the Yankees outdrew the Giants in their own Polo Grounds, and the jealous Giants evicted them after the 1922 season. The Yankees' new home in the Bronx—within walking distance of the Polo Grounds—opened in 1923, *the* showplace of baseball and destined to become the most famous sports arena in America: Yankee Stadium.

No one doubted that the Babe would raise the home run bar. In 1921, he hit 59 for yet another major-league record. Six years later came the most magical season of all for Ruth and the Yankees. Just as McGwire and Sosa would push each other to greater heights in 1998, so it was with Ruth and Gehrig in 1927.

For the first time, Ruth had a serious challenger to the home run crown he virtually owned in the '20s—Lou Gehrig, who was on the same team. When the young upstart started hitting home runs with frequency, it only inspired Ruth more. The summer of 1927, the two put on a home-run race that seized the attention of an entire country. And what a race it was.

The Yankees, on their way to another pennant with their fabled "Murderers' Row" machine, were almost a second consideration to what one newspaper termed the "Great American Home Run Derby."

For the first time, Ruth had a serious challenger to the home run crown he virtually owned in the '20s—Lou Gehrig, who was on the same team.

Starting in April and into September, Ruth and Gehrig were neck-and-neck. One day Ruth was on top. The next, Gehrig.

On September 2, Gehrig hit two home runs for his 42nd and 43rd. However, the sizzling Ruth hit his 44th to stay one ahead of his equally hot teammate.

On September 6, the two were tied at 44 when the Yankees pulled into Boston for a doubleheader with the Red Sox. In the fifth inning of the first game, Gehrig hit No. 45. One up on Ruth.

Back came the Babe, with homers No. 45 and 46; then in the second game, No. 47. The next day, he hit two more, and Gehrig was out of the race. Ruth finished with 60 homers to 47 for Gehrig, establishing a standard that took 34 years to break. (And even then, Roger Maris' 61 needed an asterisk because he accomplished the feat in a longer season.)

Though Ruth started his major-league career with the Boston Red Sox and ended it with the Boston Braves, he will always be remembered as a New York Yankee and the savior of baseball—and as an American hero of almost mythic proportions.

In 1998, the sport again needed a hero. It got two—Mark McGwire and Sammy Sosa. Baseball heroes come in all sizes and shapes. McGwire was 6-foot-5, 245 pounds. Sosa was built closer to the ground, an even six feet and 200 pounds. Like Ruth, they were at the right place at the right time. And, shades of Ruth-Gehrig, their home run race captured the imagination of an entire nation and sparked renewed interest in a troubled game.

"It's good to get the focus back on baseball, the way it used to be," said outfielder Ray Lankford of the St. Louis Cardinals. "I think everyone—the players and the fans—got caught up the last few years looking at the financial end of it."

Who didn't know about the Great Home Run Race? Everyone was talking about it, from kids on the street to world leaders. Every day they asked the same question: Did he do it? They meant either McGwire or Sosa hitting a home run. And it continued non-stop from the start to the end of the 1998 season with the two locked in the most compelling individual baseball drama in modern times.

Sosa's story began in poverty. Born Samuel Peralta Sosa on November 12, 1968, Sosa's father died when Sammy was only seven years old. Growing up in the Dominican Republic, he lived with his widowed mother and six siblings in a two-unit converted hospital building. To help his mother buy food and necessities for the family, Sosa shined shoes, washed cars and sold oranges. He had no

In 1998, the sport again needed a hero. It got two— Mark McGwire and Sammy Sosa.

Who didn't know about the Great Home Run Race? Everyone was talking about it, from kids on the street to world leaders. Every day they asked the same question: Did he do it?

formal baseball training until he was nearly 14. He did play, though—using a crushed milk carton for a glove and tightly bound rags for a ball.

One of the locals, who enjoyed teaching baseball to the neighborhood children, saw promise in Sammy and started working with him on an individual basis. When the weather was inclement they went to Sammy's apartment, where Sammy would practice hitting against kernels of corn or bottle caps, anything they could find. "Everything Hector did took me to another level," Sosa said of his mentor many years later.

Sosa was just 16 years old when a baseball scout had him try out and gave him a contract with the Texas Rangers. Two teams later, he was with the Chicago Cubs.

"When he first got here [in 1992], you could see he had great physical skills, but he was so raw," said Cubs first baseman Mark Grace.

Mark McGwire, on the other hand, had all the advantages. He grew up in California, the son of a dentist. If food was a problem in the McGwire household, it wasn't because they couldn't afford it. It was because Mark and his four brothers ate so much that his mother had trouble keeping the refrigerator full.

Bigger than the other kids, McGwire was a shy boy who found his niche in Little League, beginning as a pitcher and shortstop at the age of eight. By high school McGwire had developed into a hard-throwing pitcher, drawing the attention of major-league teams. The Montreal Expos selected him in the 8th round of the 1981 draft, but McGwire chose to accept a baseball scholarship from the University of Southern California instead.

An assistant coach at USC, Ron Vaughn, convinced McGwire to switch from a pitcher to a position player because he felt McGwire had the ability to become a top power hitter. After the two headed north to Alaska so that McGwire could play in a summer league and develop his hitting game, Vaughn was eventually fired from his job at USC. And McGwire felt responsible for it—"I have no doubt Ron lost his job at USC because of me"—So Vaughn continued to work with him.

With a school-record 32 home runs as a junior at USC in 1984, more than any Southern Cal player had hit in his entire career, McGwire played for the U.S. Olympic team that year. He left school to sign with the Oakland Athletics, and two years later was up in the big leagues setting home run records. In his first year with the Athletics, he hit a rookie-record 49 homers, suddenly joining a select group in the majors that legitimately had a shot at breaking Maris' home run record.

He was on his way in the 1997 season. And then the bombshell dropped.

McGwire was due to be a free agent after the season, and the Athletics didn't have the money to re-sign him. Rumors swirled that the Athletics would trade him rather than lose him without compensation. Driving on the Bay Bridge from his home in San Francisco to Oakland on July 31, McGwire's car phone rang. The rumors were true.

Goodbye, Oakland. Hello, St. Louis. Goodbye, home run record—at least for that season.

McGwire took a little time to get adjusted to his new surroundings. And then in 1998, he came out swinging. He hit a grand slam on opening day— and just kept on going. By the end of May, he had already hit 27 homers and, naturally, everyone was starting to calculate his chances for breaking Maris' record. With 13 homers, Sosa wasn't even in the same ballpark.

But by June he was. Once he had hit 33, Sosa was being mentioned as a challenger to McGwire. No, make that a challenger to Ruth and Maris.

America was in for a double joyride.

As the two rivals' home run numbers mounted, so did the media coverage and the fan frenzy. Most of the coverage centered on McGwire because of his hot start and an early pace that put him on course to break Maris' record. McGwire said he felt like a "caged animal" because of all the attention he attracted.

Every batting practice session turned into an event for the red-goateed McGwire. Opposing teams stopped their practices to watch the St. Louis slugger take his swings. Some of the old Babe magic was in the air. Everyone wanted to see how many times McGwire could reach the fences in BP. He rarely disappointed the crowd, smoking mammoth shots to the far reaches of stadiums.

July and August were hot—McGwire and Sosa were hotter.

By August 16, Sosa had finally caught up to McGwire with his 47th homer. Then he hit his 48th—but wait a minute, McGwire suddenly blasted four straight to surge into the lead, 51 to 48. Believe it or not, the two were tied at 55 by the end of August.

It was still McGwire's race to lose—or so it seemed, even when Sosa made it

Some of the old Babe magic was in the air. Everyone wanted to see how many times McGwire could reach the fences in BP.

After hitting historic No. 62 ... McGwire hugged everyone in sight. Even Sosa rushed in to join the hugfest.

tight. McGwire was the first to tie the legendary Ruth when he hit his 60th against the Cincinnati Reds in early September.

The evening before a two-game series with Sosa's Cubs, McGwire was having dinner with his father when the obvious question popped up. McGwire's father, John, was going to celebrate his 61st birthday the next day. "Wouldn't it be something?" McGwire said, referring to the possibility of hitting his 61st homer on his father's 61st birthday.

The dream became a reality as McGwire smashed the record-tying homer. As he crossed home plate, he looked up into the stands where his father was sitting and pointed.

"Happy birthday, Dad!" McGwire shouted.

No one would have bet against McGwire breaking the home run record the following night. What more appropriate time to do it than while facing his chief rival?

A sellout crowd was on hand at Busch Stadium as the Cardinals once more hosted the Cubs. The fans were all there hoping to see McGwire do his thing. Of course he didn't disappoint them. With all the pressure building, "Big Mac" sent a line drive over the fence in left to break baseball's most hallowed record.

McGwire rounded first base after hitting historic No. 62, a sea of flashbulbs popping, streamers and confetti floating through the air. So excited was McGwire that he failed to touch first base and had to retrace his steps to nudge the bag. Somehow, he found his way to home plate and as fireworks filled the sky, McGwire lifted his son Matt, the Cardinals' batboy, high in the air, and hugged everyone in sight, including the Maris family in the stands. Even Sosa rushed in from his right field position to join in the hugfest.

"What a feat!" McGwire crowed after going where no player had gone before. McGwire wasn't finished.

Neither was Sosa, as it turned out.

Back home at Wrigley Field, Sosa cracked four homers in three games over one weekend to tie his friendly rival at 62. As great as McGwire's accomplishment had been, he had held the home run record for all of 116 hours.

Now, amazingly, both had broken Maris' 37-year-old record in the same season! The scene in Chicago was no less emotional for Sosa than it had been for McGwire in St. Louis. After belting his second of the day and 62nd of the season, Sosa took three curtain calls with tears streaming down his face as the crowd chanted, "Sam-mee! Sam-mee!"

With each home run, Sosa had struck a blow for non-American players in the major leagues. It had taken a long time for Latin American players to win accep-

After belting his second of the day and 62nd of the season, Sosa took three curtain calls with tears streaming down his face as the crowd chanted, "Sam-mee! Sam-mee!"

The two of them had clouted a grand total of 136 home runs in what was being called a season for the ages.

tance in the majors, and now Sosa's popularity had crossed the cultural boundaries.

"It was something that even I can't believe I was doing," Sosa said.

Talk about a storybook season. There was plenty more drama to come.

McGwire hit one to take the lead. The next day, Sosa hit his 63rd to tie. McGwire hit two more. No problem. Sosa hit three straight to take the lead, 66-65.

McGwire and Sosa were playing baseball's version of "Can You Top This?"

Finally, McGwire took charge. He went on a tear and finished with an incredible 70 home runs, again going where no major-league player had gone before. To top things off with a dramatic flair, McGwire hit his 70th on his final at-bat in the 1998 season. Could Hollywood ever come up with a better script? Sosa had a remarkable season in his own right, finishing with 66.

The two of them had clouted a grand total of 136 home runs in what was being called a season for the ages.

"I think the magnitude of the number won't be understood for a while," McGwire said. "It's unheard of for somebody to hit 70 home runs. So, I'm in awe of myself right now."

And so was everyone else.

"The game has emerged from the grave with thunder," said Montreal Expos manager Felipe Alou, a veteran of 40 years in baseball. "You don't hear about the strike anymore. Sometimes, something has to almost die, like baseball did, for a miracle to take place. The average fan has more faith in the game now."

Welcome back, baseball fans.

THE FIRST ONE
Jackie Robinson

Branch Rickey shook his fist in Jackie Robinson's face. He shouted racial epithets. During a meeting that lasted nearly three hours, Rickey tried to think of everything Robinson might be called, every taunt that might be shouted from the stands. Or yelled from the pitcher's mound. Or muttered by the guy sitting next to Robinson on the bench. He challenged Robinson: *What would you do if you were called these names?*

Robinson, a battler all his life, didn't know what to say.

"Do you want a player afraid to fight back?" Robinson asked.

"I want someone with the guts *not* to fight back," Rickey replied …

The first meeting between Jackie Robinson and Branch Rickey is one of those timeless sports stories that has taken on a life of its own, much like Knute Rockne and the Gipper. But while Rockne's "Win one for the Gipper" speech has become a part of the American lexicon, Rickey's words were meant for Robinson's ears alone.

This much is known: Rickey, then president and general manager of the Brooklyn Dodgers, had invited Robinson, a baseball player with the Kansas City Monarchs of the Negro League, to his office. It was Robinson's understanding that Rickey was interested in starting a new all-black baseball team called the "Brooklyn Brown Dodgers."

But after walking into Rickey's office and greeting the famous baseball man, Robinson learned the real reason he had been brought to Brooklyn: Rickey planned to break the color line in all-white major league baseball and he wanted Robinson to be The Man.

If that was surprising to Robinson, he had to be shocked by what happened next. By most accounts, Rickey called Robinson every racial name in the book, and perhaps some that he had never heard.

He would have to pass the test, not lose his temper.

No matter how many players

A black baseball player was about to enter an all-white world, and he was going to fight the biggest fight of his life with his hands virtually tied behind his back.

It was Robinson's understanding that Rickey was interested in starting a new all-black baseball team called the "Brooklyn Brown Dodgers."

taunted and reviled him. No matter how many threw baseballs at his head or attempted to spike him on the base paths. No matter what they said about the color of his skin or what they said about his family. *Turn the other cheek.*

Robinson wasn't a spur-of-the moment choice. He had been well-researched by Rickey and his associates, who believed he was the right man with the right temperament to integrate baseball.

The 28-year-old Robinson accepted the assignment. A black baseball player was about to enter an all-white world, and he was going to fight the biggest fight of his life with his hands virtually tied behind his back.

The seemingly impossible mission began ...

Born in Cairo, Georgia, on January 31, 1919, Jack Roosevelt Robinson was just a toddler when his father walked out on the family and left his mother, Mallie, to raise five children. She packed up the kids and moved to Pasadena, California, to live with her brother. Robinson's mother worked at various domestic jobs, and Jackie helped bring in money by delivering newspapers, selling junk and hawking hot dogs at sporting events.

One of his early role models was his brother. Mack Robinson became an inter-

national track star when he finished second to Jesse Owens in the 1936 Olympics. Jackie, meanwhile, was soon making a name for himself as well. He was equally at home tossing a baseball, throwing a football, shooting a basketball or running around a track. Robinson was a star athlete at every level he played— high school, Pasadena Junior College and UCLA, where he became the first student in the school's history to win varsity letters in four sports in one year: football, basketball, baseball and track.

You name it, he was the best at it. In his junior year at UCLA, Robinson averaged 11 yards a carry as a halfback for the Bruins and one sports publication called him "the greatest ball carrier on the gridiron today." When he led the Pacific Coast Conference in scoring that very same year for the Bruins' basketball team, one coach called him " the best basketball player in the U.S." After Jackie won the 1940 NCAA long jump title in track, he seemed destined for the Olympics—until the games were canceled by the onset of World War II.

When an older brother died and Mack got married, Jackie left college a year early to help support his mother. He worked in an athletic camp and played some professional football. He was returning from Hawaii after a tour with the team when the news broke—the Japanese were attacking Pearl Harbor.

Robinson was soon drafted into the Army and within a year had made second lieutenant. One day while boarding a camp bus at Fort Hood, Texas, Robinson was ordered by the driver to step to the back. In certain parts of America, segregationist policies were still in effect and blacks were regarded as second-class cit-

Robinson was a star athlete at every level he played—high school, Pasadena Junior College and UCLA, where he became the first student in the school's history to win varsity letters in four sports in one year: football, basketball, baseball and track.

izens. Separate water fountains. Separate lavatories. And separate seating in movie theaters and on buses—always in the back.

Robinson's course of action on that bus was an indication of the course his life would take. Usually a man of immense self-control, he would certainly not be passive when it came to personal rights. He refused the driver's order.

Although such segregationist laws existed in civilian life, the order from the bus driver was in violation of Army regulations. A court martial followed, and Robinson was exonerated and given an honorable discharge.

Robinson began to get his life back in order, as many Americans did at the end of the war. The country was in a prosperous post-war boom, and Robinson's athletic career was beginning to boom, too. He signed a $400-a-month contract with the renowned Kansas City Monarchs, one of the top Negro League teams, featuring the legendary Satchel Paige. The pay was good for that time, particularly for blacks, and playing baseball in front of numerous and passionate fans was fun. Robinson held up his end of the deal, batting .387 for the Monarchs in 1945.

Integration would open up a new world for the sport, with exciting new players who had created legends in the all-black league.

That was the good news. Otherwise, travel schedules were hectic and tiring and there were few places along the way where blacks, albeit baseball stars, could find decent places to sleep and eat. Even though he was one of the top athletes in an elite sports league, Robinson was distressed with the continued bigotry he found in America. But for the moment, he could no more change it than he could change the color of his skin.

What Robinson wanted during that period was simple: emotional fulfillment. He yearned for a different pace in his life and wanted to settle down with a family of his own. He already had the girl. She was Rachel Isum, whom Robinson had met when they were both students at UCLA. There was an immediate spark between the two. It could not be sub-

dued even as both pursued their individual careers miles apart—Jackie as a baseball player and Rachel as a nurse. When they at last decided to get married, Jackie
and Rachel were set for the adventure of their lives.

Little did they know that another adventure was in store for them: Jackie was
about to play the main role in Branch Rickey's "great experiment."

Segregation had always been a generally accepted part of American life, as
American as peanuts and Cracker Jack. Baseball, the so-called "national pastime," was no different. Both the major and minor leagues were closed to blacks,
a long-standing policy that began before the turn of the century. Baseball executives saw that it continued through the Great Depression and through the two
Great Wars, and through other catastrophes of the 20th century. Blacks did their
own thing with the Negro Leagues, producing such great players as Josh Gibson
and Paige while performing on the perimeter of organized ball. In a business sense,
it suited major-league owners to keep things just as they were. When their teams
weren't playing at home, they were able to rent out their stadiums to Negro League
teams, resulting in substantial income.

Still, there were some white owners who believed that allowing blacks into the big
leagues could only help baseball. Integration would open up a new world for the

*No one could
electrify an entire
stadium, and
terrorize a pitcher,
like Robinson on
the base paths.*

After the title-winning game, swarms of fans chased Robinson for blocks, and one black journalist wrote, "It was probably the only day in history that a black man ran from a white mob with love instead of lynching on its mind."

sport, with exciting new players who had created legends in the all-black league. Another by-product of integration: a new fan base that previously devoted itself exclusively to the all-black league.

But baseball as a group remained steadfastly against such change. When visionary Bill Veeck attempted to buy the Philadelphia Phillies in 1943 and bring in top players from the Negro League, baseball's hard-line commissioner, Kenesaw Mountain Landis, rebuffed him. Rickey, a visionary in his own right, knew he had his work cut out when he decided to break baseball's color line.

Rickey had been involved with baseball in various capacities, as a player, coach, manager, and owner. His genius as a developer of young talent was second to none. In the 1920s, he had created baseball's first farm system with the St. Louis Cardinals and developed championship teams. When he came to Brooklyn in the early 1940s, he already had thoughts of integration on his mind. Rickey empathized with the blacks' plight in America. In his earlier coaching days in college, he had seen how badly black players were treated in public facilities. When Rickey later worked in St. Louis, black fans were not admitted to the grandstand. He was sickened by the injustices and wanted to strike a blow against such racist policies.

Rickey also was a practical man. In the 1940s, baseball had no television revenues to rely on, and was basically a gate-driven sport. The winning teams made money. Even though the Dodgers had won a pennant in 1941, Rickey believed he could make them still better with an infusion of black talent. Quietly, he set a plan in motion to bring a black player to Brooklyn. He sent scouts to watch the Negro League teams. They generally came back with the same report: Jackie Robinson was his man.

Robinson, a shortstop, had not only batted well over .300 for the Monarchs in 1945 but fielded "sensationally" according to one national magazine. Playing for a black all-star team in an exhibition game against Bob Feller's white all-stars, Robinson cracked two doubles off the great pitcher.

Robinson signed with the Dodgers and was assigned to Brooklyn's top farm team in Montreal for the 1946 season. Rickey felt Montreal was a good place to start for Robinson to break baseball's long-standing exclusion policy. Rickey correctly presumed there would be less racial tension in the cosmopolitan Canadian city, although he may have overlooked Robinson's own team. When Robinson made a spectacular fielding play that Rickey described as "superhuman," southern-born Royals manager Clay Hopper reportedly said:

"Do you really think a nigger's a human being?"

It would be remarks like this that Robinson would have to field gracefully; these were the things Rickey had warned him about.

Robinson became a hero in Canada when he led the Royals to the International League pennant and the championship in the Little World Series. After the title-winning game, swarms of fans chased Robinson for blocks, and one black journalist wrote, "It was probably the only day in history that a black man ran from a white mob with love instead of lynching on its mind."

"I remember one time when I was stealing home," Robinson said, *"the pitcher was so angry he didn't even come close to home plate. He threw the ball right at me."*

Next stop for Robinson: the major leagues. Although Robinson's new Dodgers teammates knew he was coming, it was still a shock to some, particularly the Southern players. During spring training in Havana, there was a revolt. Some of the players circulated an anti-Robinson petition. Manager Leo Durocher heard about it and was furious. He called a midnight meeting, crushing the movement. Still, it did not stop players from expressing their passionate feelings.

On the eve of the Dodgers' opener against the Boston Braves on April 15, 1947 second baseman Eddie Stanky told Robinson: "You're on this ballclub and as far as I'm concerned that makes you one of 25 players on my team. But before I play with you … I want you to know I don't like it. I want you to know I don't like you."

Talk about pressure. Robinson was carrying the hopes and dreams of an entire race on his wide shoulders. *He just had to succeed!*

Robinson's big-league debut was historic. Despite the fact that he was the first black man to play in the major leagues in the 20th century, there were no headlines for Jackie, no sellout crowd for the Dodgers. The competition? A searing scandal involving Dodgers manager Durocher, who had been suspended for the season by baseball commissioner Happy Chandler as a result of allegations that Durocher had consorted with known gamblers. Chandler, who refused to confirm the accusations, suspended Durocher "as a result of the accumulation of unpleasant incidents in which he has been involved which the commissioner construes as detrimental to baseball." Much of the mainstream press focused on that story as the Dodgers opened the season on a cold spring day in Brooklyn.

Robinson's performance in his first game with the Dodgers was not particularly memorable, even though he played flawlessly at first base, a new position for him. He did manage to score the winning run as the Dodgers beat the Braves 5-3.

After Robinson went hitless, a reporter asked him if Braves starter Johnny Sain had a good curve. "If that isn't a good curve," Robinson said, "I'm going to have a hard time this summer."

Harder times were coming. Robinson received hate mail and death threats. Teams considered boycotting the Dodgers. Stepping into the batter's box, Robinson must have felt like one of those popup targets in a carnival shooting gallery. Head-hunting pitchers went after him with a vengeance.

"I remember one time when I was stealing home," Robinson said, "the pitcher was so angry he didn't even come close to home plate. He threw the ball right at me."

That's not all they threw. Visiting Philadelphia created some of Robinson's worst moments. Watermelons and a black cat were tossed on the field. Phillies manager Ben Chapman hurled racial epithets from the dugout in an attempt to demoralize the rookie slugger. The stream of vituperation from Chapman was so constant and so vicious, it actually unified the Dodgers.

"Why don't you yell at somebody who can answer back?" said one Dodger. It was none other than Stanky, the man who had made his dislike for Robinson quite evident at the start of the season.

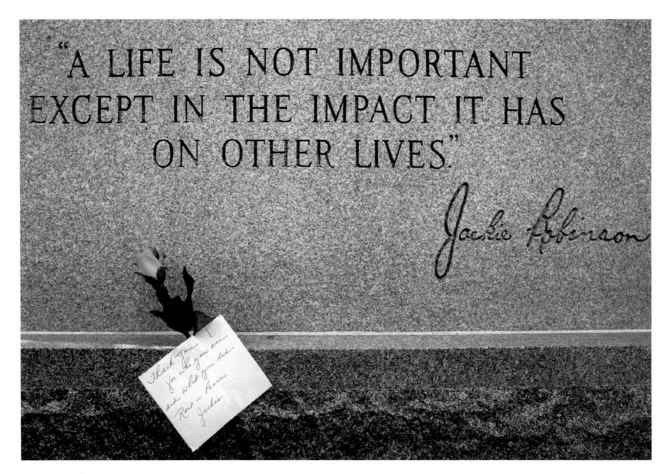

"A LIFE IS NOT IMPORTANT EXCEPT IN THE IMPACT IT HAS ON OTHER LIVES."

Jackie Robinson

His teammates started to rally behind Robinson when they realized he could help them win. He had snapped out of an early-season slump and started to tear up the league with his hitting, fielding and daring base-running. No one could electrify an entire stadium, and terrorize a pitcher, like Robinson on the base paths. Dancing off third with scoops of dirt in each fist, Robinson would slowly inch toward home, tantalizing the pitcher. "He would actually yell at the pitchers, 'I'm going. I'm going. Do anything you want, pal, you can't stop me,' " said former St. Louis Cardinals catcher Joe Garagiola.

Finally, Robinson was in no-man's land, an easy out. Or so the pitcher thought. When he threw to third, Robinson was on his way home and his teammates were laughing on the bench. By the end of the year, the Dodgers had won the pennant and fulfilled a prophecy by shortstop and friend Pee Wee Reese, who said about Robinson, "With this guy we can win."

Robinson won the Rookie of the Year award, the first of many citations in his sterling career. In 10 years in Brooklyn, Robinson helped the Dodgers win six pennants and their first World Series. He was an All-Star from 1949-54, led the league in batting and was the National League's Most Valuable Player in 1949 and, finally, was voted into the Hall of Fame in 1962. It was hard to measure Robinson's career in statistics, though, because of the intangibles he brought to a game.

He had become a hero not only to blacks and all baseball fans, but to every American who valued justice. The door was open.

He had become a hero not only to blacks and all baseball fans, but to every American who valued justice. The door was open.

THE GREATEST
Muhammad Ali

He stood over the fallen body of Sonny Liston, glowering, screaming at his opponent to get back up "and take some more whuppin'!" Vintage Muhammad Ali.

He sat slumped in the back of the private bus, napping while dozens of journalists told stories about his glory days.

Aging Muhammad Ali.

He beckoned to Jeremiah Shabazz, one of his assistants for more than a quarter-century, as if in desperate need of aid. When Shabazz came close enough, he reached out and tickled his longtime friend, who convulsed in laughter.

Float like a butterfly, sting like a bee Muhammad Ali.

Even if Ali wasn't the best boxer ever, or the most entertaining showman, or the most influential religious and social messenger, or the fairest face or the finest sportsman of the 20th century, he certainly combined elements from each category. He proclaimed himself "The Greatest," whether in rhyme in his early years as boxing's rising star and youthful champion, or through his deeds in later years, when Parkinson's disease attacked his senses. And it was difficult to argue with him.

For the final four decades of the century, Ali might have been the most famous person on Earth. In the sports world, only Pele could offer any challenge. No politician or pope, no astronaut or actor, no military figure or musician—no man or woman—had Ali's lasting power.

When asked if anyone could rival his fame, Ali once said, "Maybe Elvis." Pondering the question a moment longer, he added, "If he came back."

Ali never left.

"There have been very few men in any endeavor who have made the impact of Muhammad Ali," Howard Cosell once said. "This is a man who joined the Nation of Islam, cast off his given name, defied the U.S. government and its impossible war, and was despised for doing all of those things.

"Yet, here is a man who has become beloved by people everywhere, a great man, a great leader of astounding significance. No other man approaches the status Ali has realized, nor likely will any man do so."

Born Cassius Marcellus Clay Jr. on January 17, 1942 in Louisville, Kentucky, he hardly seemed destined to have a profound impact on America. In fact, some people who knew young Cassius said he was quiet, withdrawn, even a bit shy.

By 1960, he also was a fiend with his fists in a boxing ring. Although he hadn't mastered many of the fundamentals of the "sweet science"—indeed, blessed with such speed and agility, Ali never would bother with the basics of defense— he was an amateur phenom, winning 100 of 108 bouts.

The son of a sign painter, Clay didn't come by boxing naturally. He got into boxing by accident after his bicycle was stolen when he was twelve. In his search for a policeman who could help recover the bike, Clay wandered into a gym where the police were known to coach boxers. The atmosphere hooked him immediately.

Working his way through the amateur ranks, he twice won the national Golden Gloves and the national AAU titles. Backed by an heir to the Reynolds aluminum foil empire, Clay trained almost fulltime to win a spot on the 1960 U.S. team for the Rome Olympics.

No politician or pope, no astronaut or actor, no military figure or musician—no man or woman— had Ali's lasting power.

"I didn't know a whole lot about the Olympics," he said. "I did know it was the next step to becoming a world champion, to getting that million-dollar contract as a pro."

Clay was dubbed the "Golden Boy" even before his dazzling performance at the Rome Games, the first Olympics to get priority television coverage from the networks. Americans would dominate everywhere in those Olympics, but nobody overshadowed Clay. A light heavyweight at the time, Clay reveled in the spotlight. He made brash predictions of victory. He darted around the ring with foot speed that would have made the U.S. sprinters proud. He pummeled opponents with hand speed usually reserved for martial arts experts.

In the finals, against European champion and gold medal favorite Zbigniew Pietrzykowski of Poland, Clay was in control from the opening bell. In an exhibition that would become typical of his prowess, Clay took apart his plodding rival—and took center stage among U.S. champions in Rome.

"I slept all night with that medal on," he said. "It was the first time I ever slept on my back, or else that medal would have cut my chest."

Clay returned to a hero's welcome in Louisville, still a segregated city, but one willing to temporarily ignore its long-established social restrictions in order to celebrate the achievements of one of its own. But would a place where blacks, in 1960, had limited access and limited freedom offer any help to him?

Clay wondered that himself. He originally sought Joe Louis, the most celebrated black champion boxer, to manage him. Louis wasn't interested, even telling Clay there was no future for "such a loudmouth" in the pros. Sugar Ray Robinson, who still was fighting, had no interest, either.

"I was wondering if anybody was willing to help the U.S. gold-medal winner," Ali said.

He claimed it was his frustration with the way a black athlete from the South was treated that spurred him to throw his gold medal into the Ohio River that summer.

But a group of white Louisville businessmen formed a management company for Clay, who thanked them by winning his first 19 fights, swiftly moving up the heavyweight rankings.

Clay wasn't pampered by his promoters, either. In three of the last four fights in that string, he stopped aging former world champion Archie Moore in the fourth round, beat solid Doug Jones in a 10-round decision, and survived a fourth-round knockdown to stop Henry Cooper in the fifth round at London—a bout that nearly cost him his shot at the title.

Cooper's left hook, his one real weapon, put Clay down, but he was saved by the bell. Trainer Angelo Dundee supposedly then cut one of the gloves and showed it to the referee as if it had been torn in the fight. While the glove was being replaced, Clay had extra time to recover, and he won the bout in the next round.

That brought Clay to Miami Beach and a meeting with the fearsome Liston for the heavyweight crown. "The Louisville Lip" was at his most boastful and

most entertaining, bragging how he would "beat the big bear like I'm his daddy" and predicting in rhyme, as had become his custom, how soon the fight would end.

"You'll lose your money if you bet on Sonny," he recited. "You'll wear a frown when Liston goes down."

Liston had destroyed Floyd Patterson in a pair of title fights, and when Clay went berserk at the weigh-in, organizers nearly called off the bout. Clay ranted and raved at the champion, even rushing at Liston while members of Clay's entourage held him back. One doctor suggested the fight be canceled, but, in years to come, it would become clear that Clay executed his psych-out plan to perfection. Loony? No. Calculating? Yes. Far from being unfit to fight, he was more than Liston—or anyone else—could understand. Or handle.

Liston was accustomed to intimidating opponents even before the first bell rang. Rarely did a challenge last beyond the first few rounds. But after Clay shook off several hard punches, he took control with his jab and movement and timing. He even cut Liston in the third round. In the fourth, with Clay still dominating, a substance later identified as an anti-irritant cream that was applied to Liston's shoulder, got into Clay's eyes. When he returned to his corner, Clay told Dundee he had to quit.

Instead, Dundee cleaned out Clay's eyes and pushed him back out for the fifth round. His vision still poor, Clay danced for much of the three minutes, but twice

"You'll lose your money if you bet on Sonny," he recited. "You'll wear a frown when Liston goes down."

snapped back Liston's head with punches near the end of the round.

After six rounds, it was clear that Liston was listing. Used to having his way quickly, bleeding and bothered by pain in his shoulder and not just a little unnerved, Liston quit. He sat on his stool as Round 7 began.

"I AM THE GREATEST," Clay screamed as he pranced around the ring, the owner of the most prized crown in boxing. "I AM THE HEAVYWEIGHT CHAMPION OF THE WORLD."

Loony? No. Calculating? Yes. Far from being unfit to fight, Clay was more than Liston—or anyone else— could understand. Or handle.

He was also a Black Muslim, and just as vocal about it. The day after his victory over Liston, Clay announced that he was dropping his "slave name," and in the future should be referred to as Cassius X. Clay had become a student of the teachings of Malcolm X, which then led to his acceptance of Elijah Muhammad as his prophet.

America in 1964 was entering a period of racial discord. It galled far too many Americans that a black man owned such a prestigious sports prize. When Clay spoke of being a Black Muslim, an uneducated segment of the population equated it with gangs and militancy and anti-white campaigns. Too few took the time to learn about the tenets of Islam.

Clay became a firebrand to many of his countrymen. And when, weeks later, he took the name Muhammad Ali ("worthy of high praise"), well, it took years before the public, the media and many of his contemporaries would accept the change.

Ali was no longer merely a superb athlete. He was a young, handsome, intelligent, wealthy, talented black man holding a significant amount of power. He was a highly publicized representative of a religious and cultural sect that made white America uneasy.

"I guess that scared a lot of people," Ali said. "Most of America wasn't interested in what being a Muslim meant or how someone who made his living as a fighter could also be a follower of Islam and the teachings of Elijah Muhammad."

What much of America did recognize was Ali the braggart, and it made those people uncomfortable.

Inside the ring, he was invincible. In his first fight as Muhammad Ali, he knocked out Liston in the first round with what some say was a phantom punch.

In his first fight as Muhammad Ali, he knocked out Liston in the first round with what some say was a phantom punch.

Although it never was proved that Liston threw the fight, no heavyweight title bout since has remained under suspicion for so long.

Ali easily vanquished Patterson, who steadfastly referred to the champion as Cassius Clay until after the lopsided bout, when Patterson admitted "Ali is a great champion." He beat George Chuvalo, Cooper, Brian London and Karl Mildenberger—hardly a who's who of boxing—before his association with the Louisville sponsors expired in September 1966. Those investors earned nearly $2.5 million guiding Ali's career, but money no longer was the fighter's primary concern.

Elijah Muhammad's son, Herbert Muhammad, would become Ali's business manager, with Ali tithing millions of dollars to the Nation of Islam.

By early 1967, while he remained an unapproachable target in the ring, Ali was an easy target outside the "squared circle." He had received an induction notice from the U.S. Armed Forces, but had made it very clear he would refuse to be inducted on religious grounds.

While newspaper headlines and editorials lambasted him, Ali firmly held his ground when his name—actually, the induction officer used Cassius Clay—was called. In a statement on April 28, Ali said:

"It is in the light of my consciousness as a Muslim minister and my personal convictions that I take my stand in rejecting the call to be admitted to the armed services. I do so with the full realization of its implications and possible consequences. I have searched my conscience and I find I cannot be true to my belief in my religion by accepting such a call.

"It is in the light of my consciousness as a Muslim minister and my personal convictions that I take my stand in rejecting the call to be admitted to the armed services."

"I strongly object to the fact that so many newspapers have given the American public and the world the impression that I have only two alternatives in taking the stand: either I go to jail or I go to the Army. There is another alternative, and that alternative is justice."

Justice? Not for three and a half years.

First, Ali was stripped of his title. He was barred from boxing. His livelihood was taken away. He was a pugilistic pariah.

To some, however, he was a hero. He stood up for what he believed, and he was willing to sacrifice everything he had by sticking to those beliefs.

"I ain't got no quarrel with them Viet Congs," was one of his more famous proclamations during his exile, which lasted 43 months and took place just as it was becoming fashionable to protest the U.S. involvement in Vietnam.

Sentenced to five years in jail for refusing to join the Army, Ali never went to prison. A series of appeals, eventually leading all the way to the U.S. Supreme Court, kept him free. But he could not fight during the prime years of his career, when every U.S. state banned him. He could not travel abroad, because his passport was rescinded.

He could, however, still be Muhammad Ali. Dozens of universities invited him to lecture. He appeared in a Broadway play, "Big Time Buck White." And, of course, he preached his religion.

By late 1969, with the nation in the midst of a maelstrom of protest over the war, Ali's stance no longer seemed outrageous. Thousands of young men attempted to avoid military service, some even leaving the country, disavowing their citizenship rather than fight in Vietnam. While it's hyperbole to say Ali led such a movement, it is accurate to mention him as an important component of the anti-Vietnam surge.

By 1970, the mood in America had changed so substantially that Ali's reinstatement actually was expected when the New York Athletic Commission, spurred by the ruling of a federal judge in the state, renewed his license on September 28.

"I know I could have taken a different stand, but it would not have been the right stand," he said. "I took the right stand."

Ali's return bout was staged in Atlanta, although Georgia governor Lester Maddox, an outspoken segregationist, desperately tried to block it. Heavier and hardly in championship shape, Ali still stopped Jerry Quarry on cuts in three rounds.

Looking very rusty—and with a title fight against Joe Frazier on the horizon—Ali knocked out Oscar Bonavena in the 15th round on December 7. Three months later, he found himself in the Madison Square Garden ring against the undefeated Frazier.

"This is the greatest event in the history of the world," said Ali, who hadn't lost his verbosity during his layoff. "Joe's gonna come out smokin' and I ain't gonna be jokin'. I'll be peckin' and pokin' and pourin' water on his smokin'. This might shock and amaze ya, but I'll retire Joe Frazier."

"I know I could have taken a different stand, but it would not hvae been the right stand," he said. "I took the right stand."

Not exactly. Frazier, annoyed by Ali's taunting, was relentless. Ali, clearly far from the skill level he attained before his exile, couldn't hold him off. He had badly underestimated Frazier's endurance and fitness levels. By the 15th round, Frazier was ahead and Ali needed a knockout.

Instead, Ali went down from a vicious left hook that broke his jaw. Summoning up all his strength and courage, Ali rose and finished the fight. But he was a beaten man.

Make that a beaten boxer. Never a beaten man.

"You the champ," Ali told Frazier. "But we both proved ourselves."

From proving himself, Ali moved on to reinventing himself. His courage while being battered by Frazier—particularly in rising from the knockdown—helped rekindle his popularity. America was in a far more forgiving mood in the early 1970s, and Ali benefited.

"People realized just how unfairly he'd been treated and been made out as a scapegoat," Cosell said. "They admired his resoluteness."

On June 28, 1971, one month before Ali began a 10-fight winning streak, the Supreme Court overturned his conviction 8-0 with one abstention.

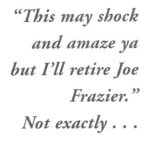

"This may shock and amaze ya but I'll retire Joe Frazier."
Not exactly . . .

Was America bitter about the judicial decision? Hardly—Ali's popularity soared in the United States.

And overseas, well, Ali was already serving as an unofficial ambassador of peace to nations in Asia, Africa and South America. In later years, he would serve as a U.S. government emissary to some of the hottest spots on the planet, always carrying a message of peace, charity and love.

Although he was winning—a loss to Ken Norton in March 1973 was quickly avenged six months later—Ali was no closer to another shot at the title. It took a 12-round decision over Frazier, plus a guarantee of more than $5 million, to get Ali in the ring with champion George Foreman on October 30, 1974 in Kinshasa, Zaire.

"This will be the greatest miracle since Christ was resurrected!" shouted Ali, a huge underdog to the fearsome, youthful Foreman, who had pummeled nearly all of his pro opponents since winning an Olympic gold medal in 1968—and waving a U.S. flag in the ring at Mexico City. "It will be the Rumble in the Jungle."

But how could Ali, with most of his skills so faded, win a rumble in the jungle or anywhere else with such a powerhouse as Foreman?

"My mind was still sharp," he said.

To fight power-house George Foreman, Ali invented the "rope a dope" strategy, an approach that confounded everyone in his corner, as well as the rest of the world.

"Boxing was my field mission, the first part of my life."

So he invented the "rope a dope" strategy, an approach that confounded everyone in his corner, as well as the rest of the world. Ali spent much of the first few rounds lounging on the ropes, allowing Foreman to blast away. Although Ali blocked most of those shots, a few got through, and it seemed only a matter of time before the heat and Foreman's blows would take a toll.

Exactly. Because after seven rounds, it was Foreman who was spent. Unable to alter his strategy—indeed, the younger fighter had no other plan—Foreman was at the fresher Ali's mercy in the eighth. With the crowd's chants of "ALI, ALI," growing louder and more persistent, the great upset was about to happen.

"I knew I had to go for the kill then," Ali said. "I couldn't give George a chance to recover."

A hard right, one of the strongest punches Ali ever threw, nailed Foreman, who went down. For the count.

Heavyweight Champion of the World. Again.

In recapturing the title, Ali had come full circle in the ring. Outside it, he had

become, in his own words, "famous beyond fame."

Maybe so, but there was more fame to come. He would go on to win the "Thrilla in Manila," a brutal war with Frazier that lasted 14 rounds before Frazier was unable to answer the bell for the 15th. Ali would lose his title to Leon Spinks in 1978, then beat him in a rematch, marking the first time a fighter won the heavy-weight crown three times.

Not until 1981, with a 56-5 record, with 39 knockouts, did Ali finish up his career. But this is not a man to be measured by numbers; measure him by deeds.

"Boxing was my field mission, the first part of my life," he said. "I predict all the preachers in the world, all the churches and religions, I will beat them in working for good. I will spread more religion and get to more people than all of the religions. I will be the greatest evangelist ever."

Still The Champ.
Still The Greatest.

In retirement, even while ravaged by Parkinson's disease, Ali has been a surpassing figure. Never was that more apparent than at the 1996 Atlanta Olympics.

Organizers somehow managed to keep secret the identity of the person chosen to light the flame and open the Games. As swimming champion Janet Evans carried the torch up a long flight of stairs toward the cauldron, Ali emerged from the darkness. Once more, chants of "ALI, ALI" rang through a sporting venue as 83,000 people welcomed him.

Bathed in a spotlight, Ali looked out over the crowd, acknowledged the cheers and, his left hand twitching badly, but his right hand steady enough with the torch in it, he ignited the flame.

Two weeks later, at an Olympic basketball game in the Georgia Dome, IOC president Juan Antonio Samaranch presented Ali with a replacement gold medal. Ali looked down at the medal, then up at the crowd as he broke into a huge grin before raising the gold medal slowly to his lips and kissing it.

Still The Champ. Still The Greatest.

THE BIRDMAN, THE SHOWMAN AND THE MAN

Larry Bird, Magic Johnson, and Michael Jordan

You're a pro basketball fan, and this is your big night. You've come home from a tough day at work and you're really looking forward to sitting down, relaxing and watching the NBA finals on TV. Except it's not being televised—at least not until 11:30 at night on the East Coast, and then only on tape delay.

Inconceivable? Nope. It actually happened in the 1980 championship series between the Los Angeles Lakers and Philadelphia 76ers. Many fans missed one of Magic Johnson's shining moments, as he led the Lakers to a final-game victory with an unprecedented performance.

"The fact that the game was not on live TV says a lot about where the NBA was then," Johnson says.

Fast forward to the 1990s, and Michael Jordan is featured on satellite TV in the NBA finals, beamed live not just to the East Coast, but to nations all over the world. Not too many missed his performance.

What happened in between?

Magic Johnson, Larry Bird and Michael Jordan.

The NBA of the 1970s had problems: with its image, with its owners and with drugs. Baseball and football were the primary sports in America, a deep-rooted part of the entertainment environment of the country. The NBA was a distant third among major professional team sports.

The league was in desperate need of a lift. Enter Magic and Bird. The flight began with those two. Later, the sky was the limit with Jordan.

"They originated the comeback of the NBA," said Jordan of Johnson and Bird. "They dominated the league with their teams. They gave the NBA a big push and got back the respect of the fans."

Bird and Johnson, Johnson and Bird. It was hard to mention one name without the other when thinking of basketball in the '80s. They were like two great actors on a stage playing off each other. There were no small parts for them. In fact, when Magic Johnson and Larry Bird first met on a basketball court, it wasn't just any game. It was for the NCAA championship.

> *"They originated the comeback of the NBA," said Jordan of Johnson and Bird.*

Johnson, the star of the Michigan State team, was expressive and enthusiastic. He could light up the scoreboard with his shots or the arena with his smile. Bird was solemn and sardonic, and sometimes even surly, but no less compelling. Almost single-handedly, he led an otherwise average Indiana State team to a perfect record and into the 1979 NCAA finals against the Spartans.

The charismatic appeal of the two stars, plus the story line of a match-up of a small-town challenger against a big-name school made it a natural for TV: David vs. Goliath on a basketball court. It was pure box-office, and it showed in the results. Never mind that Michigan State won the game rather handily, the real winner was the sport. But the two principals were the Pied Pipers with their imaginative styles.

With Bird and Magic, the pass was prologue. "Back then, all the publicity went to the slam-dunkers and the gunners," said Al McGuire, the former Marquette coach. "These two guys showed you could be unselfish and still be a star."

The game received the highest television rating in college basketball history. "It was a giant leap for basketball," said Len DeLuca, then director of programming at CBS Sports. "It catapulted the game into the '80s."

Bird and Magic's rivalry continued in the NBA, evoking memories of the titanic clashes between Wilt Chamberlain and Bill Russell two decades earlier. Just as Russell and Chamberlain had put their stamp on the center position, so did Magic Johnson with the Los Angeles Lakers and Larry Bird with the Boston Celtics make an impact on their respective positions in their own ways.

There had never before been a guard like Magic. At 6-foot-9, he changed the look of the position, and was the prototype for a whole new generation of

There had never before been a guard like Magic. At 6-foot-9, he changed the look of the position, and was the prototype for a whole new generation of jumbo-size guards in the '90s.

jumbo-size guards in the '90s. He was flashy and buoyant, a non-stop player who started, and often finished, the Lakers' fast-break game.

"I've pushed it up the court, I've dished the ball off," Magic said. "I've scored, gotten assists and rebounded. I've played guard and center on offense, and every position, seems like, on defense. And we've won."

Who could forget his performance in Game 6 of the NBA finals between Magic's Lakers and the Philadelphia 76ers? Kareem Abdul-Jabbar, the best center in the NBA, had been sidelined by injury. Johnson, only a rookie, was asked to fill in. The center position was new to Johnson, but he said he would do his best.

His best? He did better than that—Johnson not only played center, but all five positions. The result: 42 points, 15 rebounds and 7 assists as the Lakers beat the 76ers 123-107 for their first world championship since 1972.

It was the defining game of Magic's career and one of three personal favorites on his all-time hit parade. The second was the NCAA finals against Bird's Indiana State team. The third occurred at Everett High School in Lansing, Michigan, where Johnson grew up as a gym rat and basketball junkie.

"We were picked to finish last and we beat the team that was picked to finish first in the conference," Johnson remembered. "I had 36 points, 18 rebounds and 16 assists."

That's when Earvin Johnson was given the nickname "Magic." In the pros, other catch-phrases were indelibly attached to Johnson's name: "Showtime" referred to the flamboyant style of basketball he created at Los Angeles, and "triple-double" was more or less invented by the NBA to emphasize Johnson's performances that often featured double figures in three statistical categories.

Bird, meanwhile, was the best shooting and passing forward of his time, maybe of all time. Like the great Rick Barry, the best passing forward of his generation, Bird often believed it was better to give than receive on a basketball court. His shooting abilities also reminded observers of Barry; while Barry was brilliant at the free-throw line, Bird was a sharp shooter from the 3-point line.

In fact, he virtually owned the 3-point shooting title at all-star games. His opponents were often beaten before the first shot, psyched by the intimidating prospect of going up against Boston's blond bomber. At one all-star game, Bird taunted his competition in the locker room with the crack, "All right, who's playing for second?"

Bird had a well deserved reputation for hard work, practicing strenuously for hours before game time. One season on the very last day, an opposition player showed up early at Boston Garden for a game. He wanted to see if all the stories were true about Bird's work habits.

"I'm here two hours before the game, where's Bird?" the player asked.

"Oh, you missed him," an usher said. "He's already done. He's upstairs running laps."

"It would be a different game for me if he was gone," Magic once said of Bird. "He's my measuring stick."

Bird had been at it non-stop since his days at Springs Valley High School in French Lick, Indiana, a small town primarily known as the birthplace of ketchup. "I'd say my vision, my court awareness and my height are God-given," Bird said. "Everything else I've worked my butt off for."

A defining moment for Bird:

It is the seventh and deciding game of the 1988 Eastern Conference finals. Winner goes on to the NBA finals, loser goes home. Bird's Celtics lead the Atlanta Hawks 84-82 after three quarters.

Bird goes to work. He starts the fourth quarter with 16-foot and 13-foot jumpers from the right side. He steals the ball and drives the baseline for another basket. Next, a left-hand jumper in the lane, then a 17-footer from the right side. Now a driving left-handed layup. Finally, a pass to a teammate for another score. Bird winds up with 20 of his 34 points in the final quarter and the Celtics wind up with a 118-116 victory.

Whenever the Lakers met the Celtics the Magic-Bird rivalry took center stage. The NBA, a star-driven league, never missed an opportunity to promote the rivalry. There were other great players in the league, most notably Johnson's spectacular, sky-hooking teammate, Abdul-Jabbar, and the exciting, sky-walking Julius Erving. But no two to equal Magic and Bird. "It would be a different game for me if he was gone," Magic once said of Bird. "He's my measuring stick."

It helped that Johnson was a media magnet. Unlike Bird, who felt uncomfortable around reporters, Magic craved the attention. Bird never matched Magic's bubbly personality, but eventually recognized his own stature in the game and accepted his responsibility to the media and fans.

It also helped that these two megastars played on the two best teams of the decade. For their first nine years in the NBA, the league championship belonged to either the Lakers or the Celtics in eight of the seasons. LA won it five times, Boston three. They clashed in the finals three times, Magic's team winning twice.

But none of those "clash of the titans" games matched Johnson's battle against another foe: the AIDS virus. On November 7, 1991, Johnson announced to the world that he was HIV positive. He quit the game he loved amid his own tears and the tears of his fellow players.

His team at first had a tough time getting along without their floor leader. "I'd look over to his spot and think, 'Wait, he's not there,' " said teammate Byron Scott. "I had to keep asking myself, 'What's the play again?' "

Staying away from basketball was a lot tougher than Johnson thought. "They said playing basketball would kill me," Johnson said. "Well, not playing basket-

The best shooting and passing forward of his time, Bird often believed it was better to give than receive on a basketball court . . . but he virtually owned the 3-point shooting title at all-star games.

ball was killing me." No sooner was Johnson out of the game then he was right back in. He appeared in the 1992 All-Star Game, then sparkled for the gold medal-winning U.S. "Dream Team" in the Barcelona Olympics featuring Bird and Michael Jordan.

Getting back to the NBA on a regular basis was an entirely different story. When Johnson attempted to make a comeback with the Lakers the following fall, he was met with opposition by many players, who feared contamination. It took nearly five years and a greater awareness of the AIDS situation before Johnson finally was accepted back. In between, he had helped to raise the public consciousness with public appearances, television advertisements and a basketball company that toured the world to raise money to fight the disease. He had kept busy with business ventures and even found some time to coach the Lakers.

Johnson was welcomed back with open arms by the Lakers in 1996, four and a half seasons after he had announced his retirement. The 36-year-old Johnson led the Lakers to a victory on his first night back. "It was great" Johnson said. "It was so much fun. Man!"

Bird, who eventually became a coach, had retired by that time. But his impact, along with Johnson's, had already been felt: In the first year that Magic and Bird were in the league, CBS paid the NBA $16 million to televise its games. By the end of the decade, the bill was $44 million, and soon to go astronomically higher. Attendance at arenas climbed as well. When Bird and Johnson first came into the NBA, the league average was 11,000. By the end of the decade, it was nearly 15,000.

"They said playing basketball would kill me," Johnson said. "Well, not playing basketball was killing me."

Of course Johnson and Bird weren't the only reasons for the renewed popularity. David Stern had arrived as commissioner to end league chaos. There was financial stability with the salary cap, an end to the conflicts between owners and players and the beginning of a brilliant marketing campaign that included the merchandising and licensing of NBA products around the world. Drug testing helped clean up the league's image, and precedent-setting rehab clinics were instituted for players.

Television was used more intelligently to sell the game. Promotion of the stars was vital to the league's growth. Stern realized that basketball was not only big business, but also show business.

And then along came Mr. Entertainment—Michael Jordan, who was both.

Never before had the world seen an athlete dominate the marketing game like Jordan did. Who didn't want to be like Mike? Even Bugs Bunny did. Jordan, the movie star, had taken top billing over the cartoon star in "Space Jam."

Not only did the NBA love Michael, but huge corporations sought his endorsements for their products. Being an international star in a satellite age, he made more money off the court than on.

Never before had the world seen an athlete dominate the marketing game like Jordan did. Who didn't want to be like Mike? Even Bugs Bunny did.

When a reporter told Michael that a list showed him making $78,000 a day in endorsements alone, Jordan responded: "Really? That might be a little low." Like Magic and Bird, Jordan came into the NBA as a heralded player. He was a renowned figure after helping North Carolina to a national collegiate championship and the United States to a gold medal in the Olympics.

Not too shabby for someone who couldn't make his high school team as a freshman and was cut from the squad in his sophomore year. Finally, Jordan did make it onto the varsity at Laney High School in Wilmington, North Carolina. His growth spurt had kicked in between his sophomore and junior years.

One of Jordan's priorities as a youngster was to beat his older brother, Larry, in one-on-one. "Larry used to beat me all the time and I'd get mad," Jordan said. "But he created determination in me."

Jordan usually didn't need anyone to motivate him. Whether on a dirt court in North Carolina or on a polished court in the pros, few were more competitive. Ron Coley, an assistant coach at Jordan's high school, recalled that "nobody ever had that kid's drive.... Mike was furious if his teammates didn't play good defense—in practice."

Once at a Chicago Bulls scrimmage, an angry Jordan stormed out because he thought that coach Doug Collins had miscounted his point total.

Jordan explains his attitude by putting himself in the sneakers of his opponents: "Someone is trying to take something from me, to make a name for himself by outplaying Michael Jordan. I can't let anyone do that."

Few players did. In the NBA, Jordan quickly climbed to the top of the scoring charts and pretty much dominated the individual championship through the late '80s and into the '90s. Once the Bulls surrounded him with great players, the team climbed to the top of the league. As Magic's Lakers and Bird's Celtics ruled the NBA in the '80s, so did the Bulls with Jordan in the '90s. He was the heart, soul and guts of the team as Chicago won six championships in eight years. The only time the Bulls fell short in that period was when Jordan retired to pursue a career in baseball and then came back late in the following season and was out of synch.

Few athletes played with Jordan's intensity. Jordan kept the fans standing on

His leaps to the basket were dazzling flights of fancy, switching the ball from one hand to the other while seemingly walking on air . . .

"Air Jordan" not only became an expression relating to his gravity-defying flights toward the basket, but the name attached to the sneakers he wore.

their feet or at the edge of their seats with one dramatic performance after another. His leaps to the basket were dazzling flights of fancy, switching the ball from one hand to the other while seemingly walking on air, double-clutching or simply finding air space where none existed, or, with his tongue out as if to point the way, knifing like a shadow past bewildered opponents.

Just when you thought you saw it all, Jordan made you look again. He became his own point of reference.

Who could forget June 11, 1997?

He is too sick to play. That's the general thinking. Somehow, Jordan crawls out of bed, ravaged by a virus. What can he do in that weakened condition? Only score 38 points, including a clutch 3-pointer with 26 seconds left. Chicago beats Utah in Game 5 of the NBA finals.

Or May 7, 1989, when he hit "The Shot"?

The Bulls trail Cleveland by one point with three seconds left in the last game of a fierce, first-round series. Jordan takes an inbounds pass from Brad Sellers and dribbles to the top of the key. Defenders are all over him, including Craig Ehlo. What does he do? Double-clutching, he sinks an 18-footer with Ehlo right in his face for the winning basket.

Or June 14, 1998, perhaps the topper of them all?

The Bulls are losing by a point to Utah in the NBA finals and the clock is now under 20 seconds. Utah's Karl Malone has the ball—or at least he thinks he has it. Jordan sneaks up behind the all-star forward, pokes the ball into the open court, catches up with it and dribbles toward the basket. The seconds are ticking off, but Jordan is in control. Nineteen feet from the basket, he fakes out Bryon Russell, dribbles around him, pulls up and lets one go from 17 feet with 5.2 seconds left. Basket! The Bulls win their sixth championship in eight years. Oh, and Jordan had scored 45 points.

"The moment started to come, and once you get the moment, you see the court and you see what the defense wants to do," Jordan said, recalling that shot. "I saw that moment."

And basketball fans saw Jordan in another of the moments that defined his spectacular basketball career. His career as a products endorser was equally spectacular. "I've just been fortunate that my personality has been acceptable to a lot of fans," Jordan says modestly.

How acceptable? How about $100 million in one year? That's what a sneaker company pulled in on Jordan's new line. The company only expected to make $3 million in three years. "Air Jordan" not only became an expression relating to his gravity-defying flights toward the basket, but the name attached to the sneakers he wore.

Jordan transcended his sport to become an American export as well-loved as Mickey Mouse, even in countries where basketball isn't popular.

If it hadn't been for Michael Jordan, "Just do it," would not have become a world famous-marketing slogan. And Jordan, an athlete for the ages, indeed has done it like none before him.

THE OTHER BABE
Babe Didrikson Zaharias

I t's a wonder that some wise-guy promoter didn't come up with the idea of combining all the sports that made Babe Didrikson Zaharias an American icon. Say driving a golf ball off the tee and running it down before it landed, then hitting it out of the stadium for a home run.

Improbable? Babe was the one woman who could have done it. She simply was the greatest female athlete of her time, perhaps of all time, and her impact on the way women's sports were regarded was tremendous.

Babe's resume rivals that of Jim Thorpe, Bo Jackson, Deion Sanders or any of the other multi-sport phenoms of the 20th century. But it is not the Olympic gold medals and the dozens of golf victories that make her so significant. She was a breakthrough athlete, one whose achievements cleared a path for those who would follow.

Voted the top woman's athlete of the half-century by the Associated Press—she also won the AP Female Athlete of the Year award six times—Babe dominated the competition whether she was running races, shooting baskets or sinking putts.

During a golf exhibition, she would invite the crowd to "step up real close, because today you're looking at the best." She'd pound out booming drives down the fairway and turn to the men in the crowd and say, "Don't you wish you could hit a ball like that?"

At fourteen, she got the nickname "Babe" because she could hit a baseball farther than any of the boys she played against.

Everyone wished they could. And all the women who wished they could gain acceptance for their athletic prowess used Babe as their model and their rallying point.

George Schepps, an adviser and coach for Babe who died recently at the age of 98, had no doubts about her talent or her importance.

"Babe was the greatest athlete I've ever seen, man or woman," Schepps said. "She came along at a time when there wasn't a lot of respect for women in sports, and she made it acceptable. There are a lot of people who believe if it wasn't for Babe, women's sports wouldn't be what they are today."

During a golf exhibition, she would invite the crowd to "step up real close, because today you're looking at the best." She'd pound out booming drives down the fairway and turn to the men in the crowd and say, "Don't you wish you could hit a ball like that?"

Babe also made some big changes in her own biographical data. Born Mildred Ella Didriksen, she later anglicized the Norwegian spelling of her last name to Didrikson. Although there is no disputing that she grew up in Beaumont, Texas, in a 1955 biography, Babe gave her birthdate as June 26, 1914 when in fact the year was 1911.

Whatever the case, Babe didn't need to rearrange the facts. She was the best at everything she did when it came to sports, beginning her career on a backyard gym built by her father, Ole, a skilled carpenter who raised his children to be physically fit.

As a child, Babe excelled in basketball, often challenging classmates—boys and girls—to free-throw shooting contests. Naturally, she won nearly all of them, sometimes resorting to trick shots to keep things interesting. At fourteen, she got the nickname "Babe" because she could hit a baseball farther than any of the boys she played against. She was fiercely competitive and not afraid to brag about her accomplishments. How could she resist? She was good at everything: volleyball, tennis, softball, baseball, billiards, swimming—she was generally considered the best athlete in her hometown of Beaumont.

Yet this athleticism alienated her from the other teenage girls in town, who derisively called her "Tomboy." Or worse.

"That just made me want to do even better," she said. "I wanted to prove myself against everyone."

Which meant earning All-State honors on the boys' basketball team.

At the 1930 state championship game in Houston when she was a junior in high school, Babe was "discovered" by Col. Melvin McCombs, director of women's athletics for the Employers Casualty Insurance Company of Dallas.

In that first year of the Great Depression, with few opportunities for women to play collegiately and none professionally, Babe had to make a tough decision about her future. She dropped out of school to join the firm's Golden Cyclones.

It was while playing for the Cyclones that Babe found the first of her true callings—on the track. A women's team was formed by McCombs, who, upon seeing Babe's skills as a runner and jumper and thrower, refused to believe she'd never formally tried any of those activities.

Babe succeeded despite her rudimentary training.

"I worked with her about three days," said John Warren, a contemporary runner of Babe's. "In those days you didn't have starting blocks on those old cinder tracks. You just dug a little hole to start out from, and what Babe was doing was digging a

"I'm going to win the high jump and set a world record. I don't know who my opponents are, and it won't make a difference, anyway."

She was a break-through athlete, one whose achievements cleared a path for those who would follow.

hole about this big," Warren said holding his hands about six inches apart.

"It was so big she couldn't get out of it. But I tell you what, she was a natural. You'd show her something once and she knew it."

Babe won 92 medals in the 1930 and '31 seasons. She led her team in Dallas to a championship in 1931; and put it in second place in that year's national Amateur Athletic Union (AAU) championships. That same year she was named the Associated Press's Woman Athlete of the Year. She won five events at the 1932 nationals (out of eight she entered) to single-handedly win the team title. She set world records in the javelin, 80-meter hurdles, high jump and baseball throw—and qualified for the Los Angeles Olympics.

With typical swagger, Babe predicted her success: "I'm going to win the high jump and set a world record. I don't know who my opponents are, and it won't make a difference, anyway."

It didn't. Her braggadocio attracted the media, and her deeds—she won gold in the javelin and 80-meter hurdles—gave reporters the material to start building her legend.

That, in turn, made women athletes more valid in the eyes of a nation that rarely, if ever, gave a second thought to allowing women the chance to compete. Women had only had the vote at that time for roughly ten years. Collegiate and professional sports opportunities for women were still on shaky ground: critics continued to feel that women were biologically unsuited for competition on such rough playing fields.

Babe continued to prove them wrong.

"Babe's records and her abilities made her someone recognizable," Evelyne Hall Adams, the Olympic contender who lost that 1932 80-meter hurdles race to Babe, once said. "That meant more opportunities for women in sports."

Recognizable had its downside, too. Babe's high profile attracted the attention of her old friends the AAU, which directed amateur sports in the United States, when she appeared in several advertisements for Dodge automobiles. Even though she claimed Chrysler had used her photo without permission, the AAU declared her a professional. At first, Babe planned to fight the decision (it was eventually reversed); instead she saw the light and went pro, hiring a manager and getting paid even more for her appearances.

In fact, in 1934, the 21-year-old Texan turned her attention to one of the highest-paying sports ever: golf. And then proceeded to turn the golfing world inside out.

Again, Babe's version of her golfing apprenticeship is largely bigger-than-life; she did not suddenly walk in having never swung a club and beat her first opponent. She had practiced hitting balls in high school, and by the time she began to take it "seriously," was already capable of driving a ball 250 yards. She won her first significant golf tournament, the Fort Worth Invitational. She also found in golf that competitive outlet all great athletes need.

"I love the competition," she said. "Not only are you playing against another player, you're playing against the golf course. Every hole is different, a new challenge."

Ah, the challenge. It always inspired Babe to greater achievements. As did breaking into a field where her wild Texas style caused the genteel participants to cringe in horror.

She won the Texas Women's Amateur in 1935, a brash victory that so intimidated the others in the field that they followed the AAU's example by asking the U.S. Golf Association to declare her a professional. The USGA agreed and banned Babe, who began doing exhibitions with men golfers, attracting huge crowds.

At the 1938 Los Angeles Open, a men's event that did not bar women from entering, Babe missed the cut. But she met George Zaharias, a 250-pound professional wrestler. They would get married later that year, and Zaharias would become her manager.

In 1940, there were still just two women's pro golf events, and Babe won both. But she didn't collect the prize money, because she was seeking reinstatement as an amateur by the USGA. She won back her status in 1944, nine years after her banishment, and she celebrated by immediately beating the hell out of everyone on the circuit without pausing for breath. She went on to win the 1945 Western Open despite the death of her mother during the tournament. The next year, she put together an unimaginable 17-tournament victory streak.

By then, she was the most famous women's athlete in America. So she headed to Europe and won the British Ladies tournament, making her a star on two continents.

"I had reached the pinnacle of amateur golf," she said. "Pro golf was still a challenge, so I hoped by turning pro, I would better women's golf by forcing more open tournaments."

Exactly. She and Zaharias founded the LPGA, which had eight members at its outset. It is now one of the premier sports organizations in the world. Babe was as influential in women's golf as Arnold Palmer was among the men or as Billie Jean King would be in tennis.

Babe never dominated the pro golf circuit. In 1952, she underwent surgery for cancer. Although she would win several more tournaments including the Women's Open in between operations, the cancer took its toll. In 1956, at the age of 45, Babe Didrikson Zaharias died.

The world, for women athletes, would never be the same, nor would women ever again doubt their ability to make it in any—or every—sport they chose. "Babe made a difference," her husband, George Zaharias, said once. "In everything she did, Babe made a difference."

She and Zaharias founded the LPGA, which had eight members at its outset. It is now one of the premier sports organizations in the world. Babe was as influential in women's golf as Arnold Palmer was among the men or as Billie Jean King would be in tennis.

QUEEN OF THE TRACK
Jackie Joyner-Kersee

She made women's running, jumping and throwing events fashionable in the years between Olympics, when, normally, only the truest track afficionados are paying attention.

This was just too much, and Jackie Joyner-Kersee knew it. No woman had ever truly challenged the 7,000-point barrier in the heptathlon, a seven-event torture that is accepted as the measurement of the world's best female athlete. There were some preemptive strikes, but nothing like what she was doing in the summer of 1986.

At the inaugural Goodwill Games in Moscow, she set a world record of 7,148 points. Weeks later, as she stood at the starting line for the final heptathlon race, the 800 meters, at the U.S. Olympic Festival in Houston, Joyner-Kersee was about to break her own mark.

"It was kind of amazing," she said. "We had been building toward 7,000 points for a long time, and to then pass it by 148 points, and be in position to do it again by even more ... I don't think anyone could expect something like that."

Not even the greatest female athlete since Babe Didrikson Zaharias.

Joyner-Kersee eased home in the last portion of the heptathlon to compile 7,158 points in the wilting Texas heat. It was a performance so commanding that it led to the Sullivan Award as the nation's outstanding amateur athlete and the Jesse Owens Award as track and field's best performer.

And it led to such fame that, like the Babe, who had been one of her heroes growing up, Joyner-Kersee would become as well known by one name: Jackie.

In addition to revolutionizing the two-day, seven-event heptathlon—that grueling marathon of 100-meter hurdles, high jump, shot put, 200-meter dash, long jump, javelin throw and 800-meter run—Jackie was the first (and so far, the only) woman to win the *Sporting News'* Sportsman of the Year award (1988). She made women's running, jumping and throwing events fashionable in the years between Olympics—times when, normally, only the truest track aficionados are paying attention.

Indeed, an appearance by Joyner-Kersee often meant increased attendance and media coverage. It became an event, something special in a sport that rarely markets its stars or its competitions very well.

"Jackie has been one of the most influential athletes of our time," said Craig Masback, executive director of U.S. Track and Field. "For all of the records and gold medals and championships she has won, she has been just as important as a role model and community leader. Jackie is a great woman as much as a great athlete, and we in the sports community appreciate her for that and applaud her."

Applause was something Jackie heard everywhere she competed, from Lincoln High School in East St. Louis to UCLA, from national championships to the Goodwill and Pan Am Games and, of course, the Olympics.

Like her childhood idol, Joyner-Kersee excelled in several sports early in life. Born in East St. Louis, Illinois in 1962, Jackie was a renowned and versatile athlete before she'd even finished high school. At 18 years old, she was invited to the 1980 Olympic trials as a senior, where she finished 8th in the long jump.

That same year, offered a track scholarship at UCLA, Jackie turned it down in favor of basketball, as a four-year starter for the Bruins. Had she stuck with basketball, Jackie might have made her mark in the Olympics on the court. Instead, she combined her speed, strength, leaping ability, discipline and dedication to training and used them all to dominate track and field.

At the 1984 L.A. Olympics, where the five-event pentathlon expanded to become the seven-event heptathlon, Jackie, by then a two-time U.S. heptathlon champion, won a silver medal—and placed fifth in long jump. The next year, she won the Broderick Cup as the nation's outstanding female collegiate athlete and graduated from UCLA in the top 10 percent of her class with a history degree.

Offered a track scholarship at UCLA, Jackie turned it down in favor of basketball, as a four-year starter for the Bruins.

No woman had ever truly challenged the 7,000-point barrier in the heptathlon, a seven-event torture that is accepted as the measure of the worlds's best female athlete.

Then, with her incredible 1986 performances in Moscow and Houston, Jackie began *making* history.

She received the Owens award again the next year, setting a world mark in the long jump at the world championships, where she also took the heptathlon crown. Jackie was just about unbeatable heading to the 1988 Seoul Games, and she won the heptathlon and the long jump, establishing herself once and for all in a class with the Babe.

For the next four years, Jackie continued to roll through the competition, climaxing that period with a heptathlon gold at the 1992 Barcelona Olympics. By then she'd begun to slow down a bit: she was 30 years old, and known all over the world.

"It's still funny to me, having people in airports say, 'Hi, Jackie,' " she said of her notoriety. "It's like suddenly having millions of close friends."

After retiring at 36, Joyner-Kersee went back to her hometown to change the face of an entirely different arena—East St. Louis, where she began to help rebuild what has been called "the worst ghetto in America."

Jackie and husband-coach Bob Kersee established a charitable foundation that raised nearly $7 million to build a community center to replace the one where she played as a child. The Jackie Joyner-Kersee Youth Foundation, a haven to 14,000 youngsters in East St. Louis and surrounding communities, was the centerpiece of that foundation's work.

Quite a long jump for the little girl who once sailed off the three-foot-high porch of her grandmother's house into sand she carried off from a nearby park in potato-chip bags.

"I believe it is the responsibility of Olympic champions to give something back to the youth, to the public," Jackie said. "It's our duty.

"I believe it is the responsibility of Olympic champions to give something back to the youth, to the public," Jackie said. "It's our duty.

"My main goal was taking care of home first, providing them with an opportunity, because there's no recreation centers in the area. I always go back, and even though the city has problems, I always feel grateful to be a part of East St. Louis."

She's grateful, too, for the trail blazed by Didrikson Zaharias and Wilma Rudolph, so many years before Jackie became a difference-maker.

"As an athlete, you sometimes take things for granted. I think where I am today wouldn't be possible unless these women had paved the way for us. And I think I am very fortunate that I can reap the benefits they were not able to reap.

"It was a struggle then for women in athletics. If you were a girl, you weren't supposed to compete. Now, of course, times have changed."

The heightened skill level in women's sports is something Joyner-Kersee helped to establish. She joins the ranks of Didrikson Zaharias, Rudolph, Billie Jean King, Chris Evert, Florence Griffith Joyner and others as a champion who has raised the bar for women athletes everywhere.

BILLIE JEAN
Billie Jean King

Billie Jean King was going to give Bobby Riggs a royal spanking. She would do it for herself, her sport, her gender. She would do it in the most bally-hooed made-for-television event of the century. And for all of her wonderful achievements as an athlete, spokesperson, businesswoman and leader, nothing would ever quite top King's notorious rout of Riggs in the "Battle of the Sexes."

And nothing would give more pleasure to women athletes, from the champions of professional sports to the kids trying to get playing time on local fields throughout America. King's three-set victory on September 20, 1973—shortly after the passage of Title IX, the federal law prohibiting sex discrimination in athletics—would serve as a catalyst for equality such as there had never been before.

Oddly enough, the match wasn't really about tennis.

"It was about social change," said King, a winner of 39 Grand Slam titles, including a record 20 at Wimbledon. "It was about changing a way of thinking, about women being accepted."

"People don't realize what was going on. The women's movement was at its height. The Riggs match was like being in the vortex of a storm."

When King accepted the challenge from Riggs, who was 55 years old and 26 years her senior at the time of their match in the Houston Astrodome, she didn't need to establish any more credentials of her own. She wasn't doing it for herself.

"I felt like I had to win for everybody, for Title IX and the Virginia Slims tour, " King explained. "People don't realize what was going on. The women's movement was at its height. The Riggs match was like being in the vortex of a storm."

The middle of a maelstrom—it was a place where King would feel very at home as time went on. A spunky, attacking player in a game often defined by its gentility, King never backed down—on or off the court. Her fights off-court were usually about more rights for women in sports.

"Girls and boys should have an equal opportunity to the team effort," she said. "And that's what we need in society, to network by people and not by gender. Because I lived in a world—a very lonely world—where the old-boy network has always reigned. It's not fun. We have to figure out a way for people to start celebrating our differences. Not tolerate. Celebrate."

With this goal in mind, she helped create World Team Tennis (WTT) and has stuck with the concept through endless format changes and varying league makeups. Nearly a half-million players have participated in some form of team tennis, which, at its core, is also about gender equity.

In 1974, King became the first woman to coach a co-ed pro team, the Philadelphia Freedoms of WTT. Elton John was inspired enough by her groundbreaking work that he wrote a song about her entitled "Philadelphia Freedom." King now works tirelessly to raise funds for the singer's AIDS Foundation.

She has been a willing teacher, both formally and informally, and a winning coach. As the captain of the Fed Cup team—a women's event similar to the men's Davis Cup—King has aided the development of young American players.

And has anyone been more honored in her career? The list of King's off-court awards is as impressive as anything she won at Wimbledon, Forest Hills or Roland Garros: Induction into the International Tennis Hall of Fame in 1987, and the National Women's Hall of Fame in 1990; the March of Dimes 1994 Lifetime Achievement Award for her commitment to helping others; the Elizabeth Blackwell Award for her pioneering efforts in tennis and advocacy of women's equity in athletics; inclusion on *Life* magazine's list of 100 most important Americans of the century. The Chase Championships even named their season finale trophy in King's honor.

But Billie Jean Moffitt started out with many of the same obstacles facing her as any young female athlete growing up in the conventional 1950s. She was discouraged from playing softball as a teenager, and encouraged to take up the more ladylike game of tennis. As a youngster, she developed an eating disorder—binge eating—that has plagued her throughout her career. In 1995, she checked into a clinic in Philadelphia for treatment. "I was 51," King recalled, "surrounded by all these skinny teenagers who were starving themselves to death." By publicly confronting her problem as an adult, she provided a role model for others who needed a push to deal with similar problems.

During the early days of her tennis career, she was often denied travel money by local tennis officials, while she watched boys her age receive financial support.

"Time after time, they just hit you with these inequities," said King. "It piles up, and you never can back down from fighting it." In 1970 it had piled up just a little too much, and King led a fight for more equitable prize money for women with a highly publicized boycott of a tournament in Los Angeles—a tournament that offered $12,500 to its male winners, $1,500 to women. King's group set up an alternative tournament that was the foundation for the Women's Tennis Association and the Virginia Slims Tour. Later, in 1973, discovering that Ilie Nastase had received $15,000 more than she had for winning the '72 U.S. Open, King threatened not to play that year if the prize money wasn't equal;

Elton John was inspired enough by her groundbreaking work that he wrote a song about her entitled "Philadelphia Freedom."

In 1973, discovering that Ilie Nastase had received $15,000 more than she had for winning the '72 U.S. Open, King threatened not to play that year if the prize money wasn't equal . . .

subsequently, the U.S. Open became the first major tournament to offer equal prize money.

One of King's biggest fights was not on, but in court. In 1981 she was sued for support by traveling companion and hairdresser Marilyn Barnett, who claimed King owed her restitution for the seven years during which they had been lovers. Though King initially denied the allegations, she finally decided on a different course of action.

At a news conference before an overflow crowd in Los Angeles, King admitted to the liaison. "I think that shocked the media, because they weren't prepared to hear that," she said. "There wasn't even one follow-up question. I think they respected the way I told the truth."

Husband Larry—whom Billie Jean married in 1965 (they divorced in 1987) and always credits with turning her into a feminist—was completely supportive of his wife throughout the trial. She won the case, but at the cost of many of her endorsement deals; most of her corporate sponsors, she said, dropped her as a result of the litigation.

Nothing, though, could subtract from King's incredible playing record that featured the No. 1 singles ranking five times; the top ranking in doubles with Rosie Casals 12 times; the first $100,000 season for a woman athlete ($117,000 in 1971, which would translate to several million dollars today); four U.S. Open singles championships and six Wimbledon singles championships; and a tournament victory at the age of 39 years, 6 months, the oldest anyone has won on the women's tour.

Yet the match she will always be most remembered for is the one she played in 1973, when she took up Bobby Riggs' challenge.

Riggs, the ultimate "male chauvinist pig." Riggs, who had just beaten Australia's revered star, Margaret Smith Court, King's main rival early in the American's career. Riggs, whose easy victory over Court on Mother's Day threatened to set women's tennis back fifty years.

"When Margaret lost, I had no choice," King said. "I was very worried. I was scared. I didn't know what to expect. I knew [Riggs'] history. I knew he was one of the great players. I knew what he had done, winning the triple crown [singles, doubles, mixed doubles] at Wimbledon in 1939."

But she knew, too, that in 1939 Riggs had been in his prime. Now he was an aging self-promoter who survived on guile and a magical lob, a hustler who hyped the match with King so well that by the time they arrived at the court in the Houston Astrodome, a television audience of 90 million was tuned in to the $100,000, winner-take-all exhibition.

Riggs was carried onto the court in a rickshaw, while King rode on a gold litter supported by four musclemen. Riggs gave King a Sugar Daddy candy bar. She gave him a pig. Close to 35,000 spectators filled the stands to watch the circus.

What they saw—in two hours, four minutes—was a mismatch, with King winning 6-4, 6-3, 6-3. What they also saw was the benchmark moment for women's tennis. Indeed, for women's sports. It was a match that, for women in sports, was much bigger than the sum of its parts.

"It made women and girls think they could do more," said Martina Navratilova, who first visited America the same year King beat Riggs, and who followed King and Chris Evert as the leader of their sport. "They always knew it. This just proved it to them."

And it was Billie Jean King who proved it.

Riggs was carried onto the court in a rickshaw, while King rode on a gold litter supported by four musclemen. Riggs gave King a Sugar Daddy candy bar. She gave him a pig.

THE GREATEST ONE
Wayne Gretzky

I t was the start of another National Hockey League season in Los Angeles, but not just another opening night. More than a hockey game, it was a Hollywood event. The rich and famous, movie stars, moguls and mass media—they were all there to see "The Great One."

Wayne Gretzky stood in the passageway. He listened while the names of his teammates were announced one by one at the Los Angeles Forum. Finally, it was his turn, and, bathed in blue-white light, he skated onto the ice in the darkened arena. The fans rose to their feet, applauding and cheering wildly, and the noise exploded to a deafening level. In a sea of celebrities, Gretzky was the star of stars.

The fans were welcoming the newest of the Los Angeles Kings, who was acquired in a blockbuster trade with the Edmonton Oilers. Gretzky joined in the pre-game skate, half of his shirt tucked in, head tucked down and shoulders hunched in his signautre style—one that would soon become familiar to fans all over America.

The date was October 6, 1988, a significant day in NHL history.

Just as Gretzky had crossed the border from Canada to the United States, the league was also about to break into new territory. The shocking news had reverberated across heartsick Canada: Gretzky, the beloved native son, had been traded to a team in another country. No longer an Edmonton Oiler, Gretzky was now with the Los Angeles Kings. Oilers owner Peter Pocklington was regarded as a traitor.

While Canada mourned Gretzky's departure, the Kings spread out the red carpet for his arrival. Never a hockey hotbed, Los Angeles suddenly became "Hockeytown, USA."

No one could have envisioned the effect the trade would have on a team, a town and the game of hockey. Least of all Gretzky, a humble man who considered himself lucky to be making a good living doing something he loved best. First, last and always, Gretzky was a hockey man.

It was something he had done naturally all his life, from the time he was two years old and wore his first pair of skates. The native of Brantford, Ontario, became a national celebrity in Canada at 11 when he scored an amazing 378 goals in one season.

Six years later, he was a professional. Too young at 17 to be drafted by the NHL, Gretzky signed with the rival World Hockey Association. The WHA's victory was short-lived—the league soon folded and four of its teams, including Gretzky's

The rich and famous, movie stars, moguls and mass media— they were all there to see "The Great One."

Edmonton Oilers, were assimilated into the NHL.

Gretzky was the most precocious player in NHL history. In his first year Gretzky, age 19, tied for the highest point total in the league. At the age of 21, he scored a record 92 goals and was the first to score 200 points counting goals and assists. He did this with regularity at a time when 100-point seasons were considered a standard of excellence. Edmonton, a booming community predicated on oil, had another natural resource in Gretzky, who ultimately brought them four Stanley Cups. He was nicknamed "The Great One" and his number 99 was a synonym for "great" in Canada. It was embarrassing in some ways to Gretzky, yet he usually met everyone's great expectations.

But what made Gretzky so great?

Some said he had a "sixth sense" that told him where he should be on the ice at all times. Bruce MacGregor, the assistant general manager who was instrumental in acquiring Gretzky for the Oilers, thought of him in more human terms.

"He has the thing that unique athletes have—a peripheral vision. He not only sees things, he sees them faster than other players. Also, he has great hands and a great ability for lateral motion, stopping and turning. He's pretty elusive, tough to match up against."

Gretzky's mental game was as important as his physical game. He was like a chess master, thinking several moves ahead. "What gives Wayne the edge over other players is his total devotion and concentration during a game," said his father, Walter. "He's playing the game while he's on the bench."

When the Oilers traded Gretzky to the Kings in the summer of 1988, it was hard to remember when an athlete of that stature had been dealt to another team at the height of his career. Even when the Boston Red Sox sold Babe Ruth to the New York Yankees, the Babe had not reached his greatest glory.

In Los Angeles, Gretzky created excitement that rapidly turned into a solid trend. With movie stars setting the tone, it became fashionable to go to a Kings game. You weren't there to be seen so much as to see the greatest player in hockey, and Gretzky, with a string of heroic performances, rarely disappointed his fans. In his first year in Los Angeles (and just his 10th in the NHL), he broke the all-time points-scoring record of Gordie Howe. It had taken Howe 26 years to score 1,850 points.

Suddenly, the Kings were Stanley Cup contenders, and hockey fever gripped L.A.

For a team that, since the NHL's great expansion year in 1967, had never experienced the excitement of the Stanley Cup finals, the Kings—and their fans—had high hopes that Gretzky would lead them to the promised land. Or so they thought until one day in the fall of 1992.

"What gives Wayne the edge over other players is his total devotion and concentration during a game," said his father, Walter. "He's playing the game while he's on the bench."

In one fell swoop, their superhero was reduced to a mere mortal, sidelined with a herniated disc in his back. Doctors warned Gretzky that further injury could permanently disable him. Suddenly, the prospect loomed: could Gretzky's career be over? "Hockey has been my life since I was six," Gretzky said. "I was scared of how much I missed it."

And even when he came back several months later, there were fears he wouldn't be the same. For a while it looked that way, as Gretzky tried to find his game. In late season he finally did, just in time for a playoff run against Toronto. The Kings trailed the best-of-7 series three games to two in the 1993 playoffs. One more loss and they were out. But Gretzky, with that penchant for the dramatic, had one of his magic moments.

The teams were tied 4-4 in overtime when the Kings were awarded a power play. With seven seconds remaining on the penalty, Gretzky swooped in front of the net, took a pass from a teammate and scored the winning goal. The Kings went on to beat Toronto in Game 7, advancing to the finals. A loss to the Montreal Canadiens in the championship series couldn't diminish Gretzky's inspirational year.

The following season, Gretzky broke Howe's career goal-scoring record, the most personal of his 60-odd records. Howe was not only Gretzky's hero growing up, but a longtime friend. "Work on your backhand," Howe advised an 11-year-old Gretzky. The backhand shot became one of the key weapons in Gretzky's arsenal.

The following season, Gretzky broke Howe's career goal-scoring record, the most personal of his 60-odd records. Howe was not only Gretzky's hero growing up, but a longtime friend.

Gretzky added his own dimension, revolutionizing the center position by using the space behind the goal line to set up teammates for easy shots. With the ice his canvas, Gretzky made passing an art. His assists alone soon eclipsed the entire point total of Howe, the NHL's longtime career scoring leader until Gretzky shot past him.

While Gretzky's incredible point totals are well documented, as well as his brilliant play in international tournaments, there is no telling how many fans he has added for hockey in the U.S. and abroad. With his gentlemanly play and good-natured accessibility, he has been hockey's greatest goodwill ambassador. He popularized the sport in the United States as no player before him, giving rise to new fan bases in warm-weather sites.

Long after Gretzky had left Los Angeles for other NHL destinations (St. Louis and New York), his impact could be seen with two new franchises in California, two in Florida, and others in Texas, Tennessee and North Carolina, with more on the way. With many of its teams in new corners of America by the late '90s, the NHL became a more attractive product for network television.

No. 99 finally called it a career in '99 after playing 21 years as a professional. His NHL statistics were staggering, perhaps even untouchable: 894 goals and 1,963 assists for 2,857 points—1,007 more than runnerup Howe while playing five fewer seasons!

A man of great humility, Gretzky is amazed by it all. But no more amazed than those who have watched him lift his teams and a league to his level and beyond.

With the ice his canvas, Gretzky made passing an art.

THE BLACK PEARL
Pele

When you're granted an audience with the Pope and he's apprehensive about meeting you, it's likely that you have reached the top of your form in your field. Pope Paul had long been in awe of soccer great Pele. Before they met in 1966, the pontiff warned the equally anxious Pele not to worry: "I am more nervous than you, having this opportunity to meet the great Pele, someone I have wanted to meet for many years."

Why this kind of awe? Because certain athletes attain the almost unimaginable in their sports. And then they go beyond even that.

Pele was such an athlete, the greatest of all players in the most popular of all sports, one who had set records that never will be matched, creating a level of excitement for spectators and peers that no one else ever approached. Yet he moved far beyond even those on-field achievements by becoming soccer's world ambassador. Pele became an icon even in nations where soccer games were not akin to religious experiences.

"The people, I love the people. And they seem to love Pele."

"The people," Pele says, with that infectious grin that could light up the entire World Cup—and did four times as he led Brazil to three championships—"I love the people. And they seem to love Pele." They seemed to love Pele everywhere in the world, from soccer-mad nations in South America, Europe and Africa to the previously uninitiated in Asia and the Pacific Rim.

And, of course, in the United States.

During his first trip to the U.S. in the early 1970s, soccer was still a minor sport professionally. Despite its low profile, Pele almost instantly became a sporting hero and a national treasure. His appearances at the White House, when he kiddingly explained to President Gerald Ford the differences in "American football and world football," a guest spot on "The Tonight Show" with Johnny Carson, an emotional farewell game at Giants Stadium involving the two most important club teams of his career—everywhere he went, Pele made headlines.

Even the horrors of civil war ceased when Pele arrived—Nigeria and Biafra honored a 48-hour armistice so that both sides could watch when Pele went to Nigeria to play a match in the late '60s.

"I often have thought of myself as a very lucky man who was able to play a game well and then had people want to watch me play," he says. "And to spend my life traveling the world to play and teach and talk about football, about soccer, and to see the children playing the beautiful game has been a dream come true.

"When you call me an ambassador for my sport, I say that is a wonderful thing for me to hear."

Pele has had three careers: the world's greatest player while in Brazil; the centerpiece of the popularizing of soccer in the previously unconquered United States; and the globe-trotting messenger of goodwill and cooperation through sports. He was the 1978 recipient of the International Peace Award, and in 1980, he was named Athlete of the Century. In 1993 he was inducted into the United States Soccer Hall of Fame.

Quite a life for a man who grew up in poverty.

Born Edson Arantes do Nascimento in 1940, Pele spent most of his early childhood in a small village in Brazil called Tres Coraçoes. His father, Dondinho, a professional soccer player whose career was plagued by injuries, moved his family to Bauru in Sao Paulo, hoping to find a position on a team there. Despite his failure to secure regular work, Dondinho was responsible for much of what his son learned about the sport. His family may have been poor, but what Pele remembers best of those beginnings was not the secondhand clothes or the lack of shoes or the house with heat in just one room. It was playing soccer.

He and his friends would wrap together pairs of old socks stuffed with rags and tied together with string, using this invention for a ball. They'd place sticks in the ground to serve as nets. When Pele organized a neighborhood team, it was nicknamed "Shoeless Ones," because its members played barefoot.

"Soccer is a simple game to me, and that is because as a child, we played it simply."

Although his dazzling skill, speed and the beauty of his playing were his initial tickets to stardom, it was Pele's individuality and the sheer joy he got from playing that made him the most recognizable player in soccer.

"Soccer is a simple game to me, and that is because as a child we played it simply," Pele says.

In truth, from the very outset, long before Edson Arantes do Nascimento took the nickname Pele, there was nothing simple about the way he played soccer. There was a beauty to his game, a grace in the way he dribbled the ball, a precision to his passes, an elegance to his gait—even before he was discovered by Waldemar de Brito, coach of the Bauru city team.

Pele was 11 when he joined Brito's club, and he soon led it to a junior championship. And another. And another. That led to a tryout at 15 with the Santos Football Club, one of the premier professional teams in Brazil, and he made their junior team—temporarily. While on loan to another top team, Vasco de Gama, Pele dominated a tournament. Rather than risk losing him, Santos promoted Pele. He was all of 16.

Now it was time for a global stage, when the world would get to know "the Black Pearl." In 1958, not yet 18 years old, Pele traveled with the national team to Sweden to play in the World Cup. There had been rumblings in the media about this teen-ager who had risen from poverty to stardom in Brazil. It took just one goal, on a bicycle kick—a maneuver soon to become a staple of his game—for Pele to justify the hype. It took two goals in the final vs. Sweden for Pele to lead Brazil to its first world soccer title.

Of course, that was only the beginning. He led Brazil to championships in the 1962 (Chile) and 1970 (Mexico) tournaments. Although his dazzling skill, speed and the beauty of his playing were his initial tickets to stardom, it was Pele's individuality and the sheer joy he got from playing that made him the most recognizable player in soccer. Or, in other words, the planet's best-known athlete except in the United States, where soccer had yet to catch on. Even when Pele led Santos past Inter of Milan before 41,000 at Yankee Stadium on Labor Day in 1966, there was no indication he would ever have a lasting effect on indifferent Americans who seemed unable to appreciate this most popular international sport.

By 1974, Pele's career was winding down. He had played 1,363 professional games, scoring 1,281 times, breaking nearly every record on the books. After 18 years, he retired in October 1974, saying, "Football is a young man's game and I am no longer so young. But I will always be a part of the game and it will always be with me."

He had no idea how prophetic his statement was.

To sell soccer in America, the support of big business was a necessary evil. The success of the new North American Soccer League (NASL) hinged on U.S. corporations making a serious commitment, something Warner Communications was willing to do with the New York Cosmos.

Pele had already been approached in 1971 by members of the U.S. Soccer

Federation and the general manager of New York's new soccer team, the Cosmos, about playing in the United States once he had retired from Santos. At first, Pele had laughed as a translator told him of the plan. "Tell them they're crazy!" Pele said. "I will never play for anyone else after Santos!" Three years later, the offer was repeated. This time, Pele accepted.

The Cosmos offered Pele $5 million to play for three seasons in the NASL and on international tours, then spend three years publicizing soccer, running clinics and, well, just being Pele on their behalf. For Pele, who had once inspired the London Sunday Times to ask "How do you spell Pele? G-O-D," promoting the sport he had enlivened and brought to such a peak of popularity was second nature.

Cosmos games regularly drew bigger crowds than the Yankees or Mets would attract on the same day in the New York area. Top-level international stars such as Franz Beckenbauer, George Best and Eusebio came to the NASL. U.S. television discovered the sport.

"When I came to the U.S. to play, my idea was to help people understand and appreciate the beautiful game," Pele says. "It was my dream that some day the American children would be playing soccer the way they play baseball and their football. It was my dream that someday the U.S. would be the place for a World Cup, and that the American team would be as good as many other nations in soccer."

Pele and soccer, it's all you need.

Thanks to his influence, many of Pele's dreams have, indeed, come true. Soccer is the No. 2 participation sport among American youths, behind only basketball. The 1994 men's World Cup, staged across the United States, was the most profitable in history. The 1999 women's event was a huge success. Already, plans are underway in the States to bid for another men's tournament. And of course, in bringing his country into the limelight, Pele paved the way for other South American players.

Although professional soccer hit a lull in the 1980s as the NASL folded, the indoor game did well and still does. The boost from World Cup USA in 1994 led to a new professional league, Major League Soccer, which appears to have solid backing.

It's been nearly a quarter-century since Pele's final game, at Giants Stadium where he played one half with the Cosmos, one half with Santos. Of course, he scored a goal in that memorable contest, on a first-half penalty kick for the Cosmos, who beat Santos 2-1.

But it was the pre-game message he delivered that summed up Pele's relationship with the fans—and his sport.

"I want to take this opportunity to ask you in this moment, when the world looks to me, to take more attention to the young ones, to the kids all over the world," he said. "We need them too much. And I want to ask you, because I think love is the most important thing in the world that we can take in life ... people, say with me three times: LOVE, LOVE, LOVE."

Pele and soccer, it's all you need.

ONE GOLDEN MOMENT
Jim Thorpe

Imagine the Olympics without the "Dream Team" No Magic, Michael and Bird … no hockey stars like the Great One … in fact, no athlete who receives a salary of any kind …

Welcome, you are entering the Thorpe Zone.

It is 1913 and you have been ostracized by the International Olympic Committee for receiving five dollars a game—a *game*—for playing baseball during a break from school.

You have to give back your two gold medals in track and field. And return all the other baubles that you received from the King of Sweden and the Czar of Russia. It doesn't matter that in the 1912 Olympics you won both the pentathlon and the decathlon, miles ahead of your competition. It doesn't matter that you're considered the greatest athlete in the world.

Now you are stripped of all your prizes and your pride has been stripped away as well, laid bare for all to see. Your name is Jim Thorpe.

So how did this all happen?

Thorpe was of Irish and American Indian descent, the great-grandson of Sauk and Fox warrior-chief Black Hawk. Born May 22, 1887, he grew up in Oklahoma on Indian land. He was born to ride and born to run. He emulated his father, Hiram, who was a horse trainer and an excellent athlete. Hiram would take his son on all-day excursions covering up to 30 miles on foot, and young Jim would have to hustle to keep up with him. They fished in the streams using long spears, hunted bear and tamed wild colts. The death of Jim's twin brother, Charlie, to pneumonia in 1897, reinforced Jim's already powerful relationship with his father.

Missing his brother and unhappy at the reservation school, Thorpe skipped out one day and ran the 23 miles back home. When he arrived, his father was upset to see that his son had cut school. Into the car and back to school they went. Hiram Thorpe left his son at the schoolhouse door and—mission accomplished—drove back home.

Imagine his surprise when he pulled up and saw Jim waiting for him. The young Thorpe had once again covered the 23 miles, over fields and meadows, and actually beat his father's vehicle home.

Thorpe's incredible athletic ability had to come into play somewhere, if it could no longer be applied to day-long hunting

> *You have to give back your two gold medals in track and field. And return all the other baubles that you received from the King of Sweden and the Czar of Russia.*

trips with his father. At Carlisle, an industrial school for Indians in Carlisle, Pennsylvannia., the 19-year-old Thorpe was walking around campus one day when he saw the track team working out. Impatiently he watched as each member attempted to hurdle the bar at 5-foot-9. Finally, Thorpe asked to try. At first the athletes stood by snickering at this Okie Indian in overalls and regular walking shoes, but their smiles vanished as Thorpe easily cleared the bar, street clothes and all.

Also watching the proceedings was Glenn Scobey "Pop" Warner, the coach of the track team. Afterward, he walked over to Thorpe and excitedly told him he had broken the school record.

"That's not very high," Thorpe said. "I can do a lot better in a track suit."

And he did. Wearing a Carlisle track suit, Thorpe won the high jump at the famed Penn Relays in 1908. He also made his impact on the football team. The Carlisle team was playing Pennsylvania when suddenly its regular halfback was injured and Jim was called off the bench to substitute. He ran 65 yards for a touchdown. That wasn't good enough. He followed with an 85-yarder for another TD as the underdog Indian team knocked off the high and mighty Ivy Leaguers.

At first the athletes stood by snickering at this Okie Indian in overalls and walking shoes, but their smiles vanished as Thorpe easily cleared the bar. . .

Thorpe left Carlisle to play semipro ball in North Carolina for $5 a game, then returned to his old school two years later to play football in 1911 and train for the 1912 Olympics. In those days, Harvard was considered the Notre Dame of football. Small, ill-equipped and undermanned Carlisle didn't stand a chance against the unbeaten powerhouse. Or so everyone thought. Then Thorpe made his presence known. He gained 173 yards carrying the football, scoring one touchdown, and kicked four field goals as the Indians pulled off the biggest upset of the 1911 season by beating Harvard. Carlisle had suddenly become a little powerhouse, and Thorpe an All-American as opponent after opponent fell.

Soon, Thorpe's national reputation would be international. Arriving in Stockholm for the Olympics, Thorpe was about to make history. In the pentathlon, Thorpe finished first in four of the five track and field events, then capped that performance by winning the 10-event decathlon, destroying all competition. His point total of 8,412 out of a possible 10,000 was unheard of. At the award ceremonies, King Gustav of Sweden awarded Thorpe the gold medals, a laurel wreath and trophies.

"You know, Chief," Thorpe said, "the King of Sweden gave me those trophies. He gave them to me. But they took them away from me. They're mine, Chief, I won them fair and square."

"Sir, you are the greatest athlete in the world," Gustav said.

"Thanks, King," Thorpe is said to have replied in all innocence.

He was euphoric, the only thing missing from the triumphs being his mother and father, who had died a few years earlier. Thorpe wished they could have seen the ceremonies, and also the ticker-tape parade that greeted him in New York. But there was still Carlisle, where he returned an Olympic hero, and resumed his glittering college football career. But not for long.

In January 1913, the news sent shock waves around the world: The Olympic Committee ordered Thorpe to return the gold medals and trophies he won at the 1912 Games. Thorpe had committed the unpardonable sin of taking money to play a sport. Under Olympic rules, he was considered a professional. It didn't matter that the sport was baseball, and not track and field, and it didn't matter that the sum was very small. Jim Thorpe was disgraced.

And devastated. He begged the committee not to take his prized medals away, pleading with them in a letter: "I was not wise in the ways of the world and did not realize this was wrong, and that it would make me a professional in track sports. …" But the Olympic investigation, which started and ended with Thorpe (though other athletes at the time were guilty of the same offenses under fake names), was merciless. Thorpe's records were deleted from the Olympic record books and the athletes who had finished far behind him in the point totals suddenly became gold medal winners.

Although he continued to play sports professionally, an incident a few years later when he was playing baseball with the New York Giants showed the extent of his heartbreak over the decision. One late night, Giants catcher Chief Meyers was awakened by Thorpe. His roommate was crying. "You know, Chief," Thorpe said, "the King of Sweden gave me those trophies. He gave them to me. But they took them away from me. They're mine, Chief, I won them fair and square."

Summers were made for pro baseball, and falls for football as Thorpe signed on with the Canton (Ohio) Bulldogs as player-coach. His first few games were against the Massillon Tigers, a team that featured a young football genius by the name of Knute Rockne.

Their paths crossed immediately when Rockne tackled Thorpe on his first few runs. Thorpe was furious. On the very next play, he ran straight at Rockne, knocking him unconscious. As Rockne came to, he saw Thorpe bending over to help him up.

"That's better, Knute," Thorpe said, pounding Rockne on the shoulder. "These people want to see Big Jim run."

And run he did. Thorpe loved football more than any sport because he liked to play rough. He enjoyed physical contact and didn't mind dealing out punishment as he carried the ball. Thorpe did it all for the Bulldogs: run with power, pass, drop-kick, punt and place-kick. He was the first glamour player in pro football, his name usually appearing ahead of the team name on placards. Before Thorpe showed up, Canton had averaged 1,200 fans a game. When Thorpe played in Canton's first game with Massillon, a crowd of 8,000 turned out.

In the '20s, during the so-called Golden Age of Sports, the hero mythology was building in America. Alongside such names as Babe Ruth, Jack Dempsey and Rockne, Jim Thorpe was a real force. Even though his name had been tainted by the Olympic disaster, he remained a hero to many Americans who sympathized with his plight. Even without his gold medals, his name was still as golden as the others in many respects.

When pro football began getting serious about itself in the early '20s, it was Thorpe, the football hero, that a new loosely formed league turned to for help. Thorpe was asked to be the first "president" of the American Professional Football Association, which later would become the National Football League. The league wanted Thorpe's name on its stationery to lend credence to its presence.

His personal life, meanwhile, was troubled. Thorpe's infant son had died and his wife had divorced him. Finally, his great athletic skills also deserted him and he retired from pro football in 1929 at the age of 41. He was a man in search of himself, in the back of whose mind was the hope he could somehow reclaim those lost gold medals from the Olympics. How, he didn't know. It was a crucial part of his life that was missing: the physical evidence of his greatness as an athlete.

It was a difficult time to be out of work, right after the Great Depression.

Thorpe was asked to be the first "president" of the American Professional Football Association, which later would become the National Football League.

In 1982, the International Olympic Committee voted to return Thorpe's gold medals, giving two replicas to each of his seven children and re-entering his records in the Olympic books.

Thorpe picked up odd jobs and eventually drifted out to Los Angeles, finding work as a construction laborer and occasionally playing an Indian in the movies. When the 1932 Olympics came along, it was rumored that he couldn't afford to buy a ticket. Hearing of Thorpe's plight, U.S. vice president Charles Curtis invited him to sit in the presidential box at the Olympic stadium, where upon his appearance, Thorpe received a standing ovation from the crowd of 105,000.

In 1950, the Associated Press voted Thorpe "Athlete of the Half-Century." Thorpe had spent the intervening years involved in Indian causes and speaking on the lecture circuit about his sports career and the Indian culture. But no one could give him what he really wanted: his coveted Olympic medals.

Public opinion was clearly in his favor. There had been campaigns to reverse the Olympic sanctions. In 1943, the Oklahoma legislature adopted a resolution by two Indian members to petition the Amateur Athletic Union to reinstate Thorpe's records. No luck.

Stories about Thorpe dying "a penniless alcoholic" conflict with his son's claims that Thorpe at the time of his death owned two bars and was working as a sports director. But one thing was certain; when he died on March 28, 1953 of a heart attack in a California trailer park, it was without having achieved his most important goal. Hearing of Thorpe's death, President Dwight D. Eisenhower acknowledged that he "occupied a unique place in the hearts of Americans everywhere." An entire nation mourned, as if losing a close friend.

Thorpe's family, including his third wife, and friends continued the mission to recover the Olympic gold. Twenty years passed before a break finally came. In a surprising turn, the U.S. Olympic Committee voted to restore Thorpe's amateur status in 1973. But why then and not before?

"Rules on eligibility were changing drastically in the 1970s," said Bob Condron, a spokesman for the U.S. Olympic Committee. "The fact that some of the things Thorpe had done were not now violations probably had a lot to do with the reinstatement."

The new Olympic rules were quite clear: You could play professionally in one sport and not be disqualified from competing as an amateur in another. Thorpe had posthumously won his battle, and popular opinion had been satisfied. In 1982, the International Olympic Committee voted to return Thorpe's gold medals, giving two replicas to each of his seven children and re-entering his records in the Olympic books.

Soon enough, professional teams were being sent to the Olympics, now a money-making machine. From 1993 to 1996, the Olympics pulled in $4 billion for its organizations and showcased the best pro talents in the world. Who didn't enjoy watching the U.S. "Dream Team" featuring Michael Jordan, Magic Johnson and Larry Bird, shown worldwide on television? Or Wayne Gretzky, headlining a galaxy of National Hockey League stars?

When Jim Thorpe was born, he was given the Indian name of Wa-Tho-Huck, meaning "Bright Path." The name was appropriate. Thorpe had shown the way.

PIVOTAL PLAYERS

George Mikan, Wilt Chamberlain, and Bobby Orr

GEO MIKAN VS. KNICKS. The marquee outside Madison Square Garden told the story as fans streamed through the turnstiles on December 13, 1949 to see the New York Knicks take on the Minneapolis Lakers.

The management at the Garden, trying to sell pro basketball in an era when colleges were the big game in town, was doing the obvious: pushing George Mikan.

It was not lost on Mikan's Laker teammates, who were used to the hype.

"George, why don't you go out and play the Knicks, and we'll all wait here until you get back?" a teammate teased Mikan as the star center dressed for the game.

Apocryphal or not, the story makes the point: Mikan was pro basketball's meal ticket and first superstar in those early days of the NBA, and even before there

Mikan was pro basketball's meal ticket and first superstar in those early days of the NBA, and even before there was an NBA.

He not only triggered the revolution of 7-footers and inspired rule changes as did Mikan, but Wilt the Stilt also raised the bar on salaries.

was an NBA. That was his immediate impact. In time, Mikan's presence would have more far-reaching effects than anyone would have guessed.

When Mikan entered professional basketball, the slam-dunk hadn't been invented. Nor had the alley-oop, or the sky hook. The fast-break was something students did after the final day of school. And sky-walking was usually applied to high-wire acts, and other circus-like activities, never basketball. The game's stock and trade was set shots and solid passing. And no shot clocks, of course.

Not to mention that the rules hadn't yet been written to accommodate a player who combined Mikan's height and mobility.

Fast forward to the '60s and meet Mikan's linear descendant, Wilt Chamberlain, a revolutionary player in his own right. Like Mikan, Chamberlain was usually the main attraction wherever he went. He patented the slam dunk and the finger roll, and was extremely well coordinated for a man his size. A one-man demolition force, he tore up the record book, and practically rewrote it all by himself. He not only triggered the revolution of 7-footers and inspired rule changes as did Mikan, but Wilt the Stilt also raised the bar on salaries.

And then there was Bobby Orr, who completely changed the level of play for defensemen in hockey in the 1960s and '70s. Orr removed the leg irons from the players who mainly stayed back and defended the goal. That's what defensemen were supposed to do—until Orr showed them the freeway.

Three athletes, two different sports, but a single result: they changed the way their games were played or perceived.

The time was the late '40s, and the world was finally at peace, except for the warring two professional basketball leagues in America: the National Basketball League (NBL) and the Basketball Association of America (BAA). As the two-time college player of the year at De Paul, and a national champion, to boot, George Mikan had his pick of the leagues.

He signed with the Chicago Gears of the established NBL for an amazing amount of money at the time—$60,000 over five years. If he didn't make it in pro basketball, Mikan felt he could go into law. He was taking courses in the

summer at De Paul.

Mikan didn't have to worry about getting a day job, even after the Gears folded halfway through the season. He wound up with the Minneapolis Lakers—and a legend began.

At the time the 6-foot-10, 245-pound Mikan came into the league, he was unique, and for more than just his height. Although there were some players his size in pro basketball, none had Mikan's mobility or athleticism. Here was a big man with strength who could pass, shoot and rebound with equal ease. Before Kareem Abdul-Jabbar's famed sky hook, there was Mikan's short hook shot—right- and left-handed. Abdul-Jabbar, born in 1947—the year Mikan played his first pro game—said he practiced Mikan's hook in the sixth grade.

Although there were some players his size in pro basketball, none had Mikan's mobility or athleticism.

According to teammates, no one could duplicate his competitiveness.

"His will to win permeated the whole team," said Bud Grant, who played with Mikan and later became a Hall of Fame football coach. "It was a great thrill playing with such a man."

It wasn't that much fun playing against him. Opposing teams tried to devise game plans to stop him, usually to no avail. Finally, the Fort Wayne Pistons figured out a way: freeze the ball and keep it out of Mikan's hands. The Pistons held the ball for most of the game and emerged with a 19-18 victory, the lowest score in pro basketball history. The embarrassing "slowdown game" forced the league to install the 24-second clock, the first step toward the explosive, high-powered game we know today.

Soon enough, the league widened the free throw lane from 6 to 12 feet and made it illegal for a player to stand there for more than three seconds. The rule was passed to prevent big, mobile players like Mikan from dominating the area around the basket. Mikan's immovable presence in the low post had forced the league to re-examine the way its game was played.

Mikan's teams won championships during a time of transition in pro basketball. In an uncertain time when franchises were either folding, moving, or merging, one of the few certainties was the Lakers. They won championships in three leagues, six in all from 1948–54. By then the NBL and BAA had folded, and the NBA was taking flight with Mikan as its primary attraction.

In the '60s, Wilt Chamberlain sent the league soaring—more points, more rebounds, more money than anyone had ever seen before. The 7-foot-1 Chamberlain was a king-size Babe Ruth. He did everything in a big way.

Chamberlain's hallmark achievement was 100 points in 1962. Less than 5,000 people saw the performance against the New York Knicks in Hershey, Pa., but millions remember it.

The game was not televised, so only the memories of the few who actually saw it and participated in it remain. It has been recounted over and over as part of basketball lore, just as Ruth's 60-homer season was a part of baseball. The 100-point game was spectacular in itself. But Chamberlain was *averaging* 50 points over an entire season. He did that in 1961-62, and it's one of many offensive marks held by the Big Dipper, considered the strongest player in the league in his time.

Chamberlain was the top drawing card in the NBA for many years and his six-figure salary reflected it. He opened the door for other players to cash in, including his biggest rival, Bill Russell. When Russell heard that Chamberlain was making $100,000, he reportedly asked the Boston Celtics to pay him $100,001.

The Chamberlain-Russell battles were legendary, intensifying interest in bas-

When [Bill] Russell heard that Chamberlain was making $100,000, he reportedly asked the Boston Celtics to pay him $100,001.

"Bobby controlled the puck for 40 minutes, and let the other 35 players in the game use it for the other 20."

ketball. Chamberlain usually won the individual battles, but Russell won most of the championships. Chamberlain played with Philadelphia then, later San Francisco, and finally, Los Angeles in his prime.

With Chamberlain's leaping ability, there was some talk at one point of raising the basket a couple of feet. It never happened, but other rules were instituted in deference to Chamberlain—among them a further widening of the free throw lane to keep pivot men from dominating the paint and offensive goaltending, which did not allow a player to touch a ball on its downward flight to the basket.

As Chamberlain's 100-point game defined his career, so did one particular goal that Bobby Orr scored for the Boston Bruins in the 1970 Stanley Cup Finals. Orr's magic moment was frozen in time by photographers: the Bruins' star flying through the air after scoring the Cup-clinching goal in overtime against the St. Louis Blues.

The goal was important to hockey, not just for winning the Cup, but for epitomizing a new way of life for NHL defensemen.

Aggressive and incredibly fast—that was Orr's game, had always been since coming out of the Canadian juniors, a hotshot prospect from Parry Sound, Ontario.

"I came in playing a different style, offensive defenseman," Orr said. "I loved to carry the puck. I always played like that since I was a kid."

The Bruins had not won a championship since 1941. Enter Orr, and Boston won two, in 1970 and 1972. Orr made hockey more exciting, and set the stage for rushing defensemen such as Paul Coffey, Ray Bourque and Brian Leetch.

There had been other puck-carrying defensemen before Orr, but none with his electrifying style. Orr's end-to-end rushes were breathtaking. So were his point totals. Before Orr came on the scene, a defenseman had never led the NHL in scoring. All he did was lead the league twice. Remarkable enough, but he also became the first player in NHL history to score more than 100 points. And he did it six times!

Orr's impact was made in a relatively short time. He was forced to leave the game prematurely due to numerous knee injuries. He had played for 12 NHL seasons, but only minimally over the last three years, finishing up his career in Chicago. He won the Norris Trophy as the NHL's top defenseman for eight straight years and accumulated 270 goals and 645 assists for 915 points in only 657 games.

Remembering one of Orr's typical games when he scored a goal, set up another and almost single-handedly killed the other team's power play by hogging the puck, Bruins teammate Derek Sanderson quipped:

"Bobby controlled the puck for 40 minutes, and let the other 35 players in the game use it for the other 20."

Pivotal players do things like that.

Orr's magic moment was frozen in time by photographers: the Bruins' star flying through the air. . . .

COMMISSIONER PETE AND BROADWAY JOE
Pete Rozelle and Joe Namath

Pete Rozelle was hardly a commanding presence when he stood at a podium. He normally wore a subdued, dark blue suit and solid tie. His receding hairline befitted a sports commissioner. Though far from conservative, Rozelle knew how to project the proper image for his office.

When Joe Namath entered a room, he was often peeling off a fur coat to reveal a flamboyant, open-collared shirt and bell-bottom slacks. He kept his hair long, a little wild. Namath also knew how to project the image he sought as pro sports' most illustrious bad boy—even if his background was more conservative than Rozelle's.

As the National Football League's popularity exploded in the late 1960s and early 1970s, these two seeming opposites were at the forefront: Commissioner Pete and Broadway Joe. They didn't achieve such notoriety together, though one memorable encounter is typical of them both.

In 1969, Rozelle summoned the New York Jets quarterback to warn him to sell his interest in a nightclub, Bachelors III, because "undesirable characters" frequented it. Otherwise, Namath would be suspended. Rozelle invited Namath to his apartment for the meeting, and the commissioner sent his young daughter Anne Marie into a bedroom, telling her not to come out until the talk was over.

But females of all ages fell under Namath's spell, and Anne Marie was no exception. "I contained myself for as long as I could," she recalled, "and then, as Joe was leaving, I burst into the room and said, 'Joe, I love you even though my father hates you!' To which my father, surprised at what I had done, said, 'So much for diplomacy and tact.'"

These were qualities the commissioner valued highly in his job. Like baseball commissioner Kenesaw Mountain Landis decades before him, Rozelle was forced to deal with several such unsavory issues. While he didn't have anything as scandalous as the 1919 Black Sox scandal (which forced Landis to suspend eight members of the Chicago White Sox for dumping World Series games), Rozelle tackled his fair share of unethical behavior.

When Joe Namath entered a room, he was often peeling off a fur coat to reveal a flamboyant, open-collared shirt and bell-bottom slacks.

Though far from conservative, Rozelle knew how to project the proper image for his office.

In 1963, Rozelle suspended indefinitely Green Bay Packers halfback Paul Hornung and Detroit Lions defensive tackle Alex Karras, two of the NFL's biggest stars, for placing bets on their own teams. Both would be reinstated a year later.

"Pete had spoken to the Lions and he called [Packers coach] Vince Lombardi to New York to present him with a summary of the results of the investigation," recalls NFL vice president Joe Browne. "Vince said, 'Looks like you have no choice. Do what you have to do and let's go have lunch.'

"Pete said one of the toughest phone calls was when [he] called Hornung to tell him that he was going to be suspended, and he got Paul's mother. She was so excited that Pete Rozelle was calling, and she had no idea for what reason he was calling.

"Pete couldn't tell her, so he said, 'Just have Paul call me.' "

That was Rozelle's style—forceful when he needed to be, yet despite the reserved public demeanor, surprisingly emotional underneath.

Browne remembered another time when Rozelle was unable to hide his feelings. Rozelle had hired the first black executive in sports, Buddy Young, who served as a liaison to the players. When Young died in a car accident and the NFL had a memorial service for him, Rozelle was one of the speakers. He choked up early in his speech and couldn't continue.

"Pete's eyes could tear up very quickly," Browne observed.

But Rozelle's eyes also saw the future as early as 1960, when—after working with the Los Angeles Rams, first in public relations, and eventually as general manager—he was elected NFL commissioner as a compromise candidate.

It took 23 ballots to elect Rozelle, a longshot choice who immediately set about leading the league to the top of the American sports pantheon.

"I think the National Football League in 1960, when he took over as commissioner, [at] 33 years old, was facing one of the most energetic, volatile periods that we've ever seen in sports—in television and all the other things," former Dallas Cowboys executive Tex Schramm said.

"He was able to bring a young man's vision, a young man's background into the role and produce a league that surpassed major league baseball and everything else to become the greatest entertainment force that we know today."

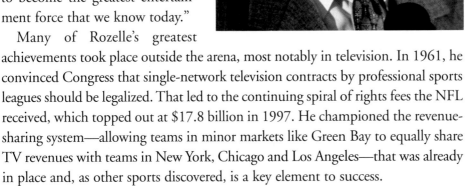

"I had about as much clout as the Dalai Lama has dealing with the Chinese army, " Roone Arledge said of Rozelle. "You knew where the power was."

Many of Rozelle's greatest achievements took place outside the arena, most notably in television. In 1961, he convinced Congress that single-network television contracts by professional sports leagues should be legalized. That led to the continuing spiral of rights fees the NFL received, which topped out at $17.8 billion in 1997. He championed the revenue-sharing system—allowing teams in minor markets like Green Bay to equally share TV revenues with teams in New York, Chicago and Los Angeles—that was already in place and, as other sports discovered, is a key element to success.

"Without it," Rozelle said, "can we even imagine the Green Bays and Buffalos competing with the New Yorks and Chicagos?"

During the bidding war between the AFL and NFL for college talent from 1960–66, Rozelle had NFL teams pledge not to sign seniors until completion of all their games. He also proclaimed that no underclassmen be drafted, a policy that stood for nearly two decades, before the courts struck it down. While he was not the driving force behind the merger, which took four years to complete after agreement was reached in 1966, he supported the work of Lamar Hunt and Schramm, who pioneered it.

And he encouraged the creation of an AFL-NFL championship game, suggesting it be played even before the merger was fully achieved. The game would become known as the Super Bowl, an apt description for its drawing power, if not for the quality of many of its matchups.

Where Rozelle made his biggest mark, though, was in changing the way Americans spent Sunday afternoons and Monday evenings.

By the time of the merger, the league already was reaping huge financial benefits from TV. When Rozelle began negotiations for the creation of Monday Night Football, he pushed to get all three networks involved. ABC Sports President Roone Arledge said he was on the defensive in contract talks with Rozelle, because "I had about as much clout as the Dalai Lama has dealing with the Chinese army. You knew where the power was." From there, the unchallenged NFL has been the hottest sports commodity on the tube.

Only on occasion did Rozelle's wisdom fail him. On November 24, 1963, he made what he long acknowledged was his biggest mistake—allowing games to be played two days after the assassination of President Kennedy.

In 1985, Rozelle received the unique honor of being elected to the Pro Football Hall of Fame, even though he was not yet retired. Accompanying him in the Class of '85 was Joe Namath.

But by the mid-1980s, Rozelle tired of the constant litigation in which professional football found itself. Although he oversaw the NFL's overwhelming victories against challenging leagues (the World League in the 1970s, the U.S. Football League in the 1980s), the amount of time, energy and resources the NFL spent in courtrooms annoyed him.

So did labor battles, which led to lengthy strikes in 1982 and 1987. Rozelle's image took major hits during those seasons—particularly with the use of replacement players in '87—but the league never backed down in its negotiations with the player's union.

By 1989, exhausted from dealing with 28 owners, many with their own agendas, Rozelle surprised nearly everyone by announcing his retirement at the winter meetings. He lived a generally private life from then on. Rozelle died of brain cancer on December 6, 1996. He was 70 years old.

'He moved the NFL from the back page to the front page, from daytime to prime time," New York Giants owner Wellington Mara said at Rozelle's funeral. "He inspired selflessness and moved the NFL to the undisputed front line of professional sports in this country.

"He'll forever be remembered as the standard by which all sports executives are judged."

"He moved the NFL from the back page to the front page, from daytime to primetime."

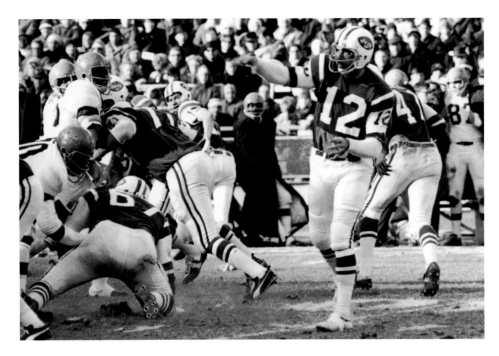

". . . I got the first paycheck. It was made out to Joseph W. Nathan Can you imagine that? . . . I got it cashed, though."

Just as Namath might be the measuring stick for the image of the professional athlete.

Before the New York Jets signed the strong-armed quarterback out of the University of Alabama in 1965, the AFL was struggling to survive its bidding wars with the NFL for talent. It needed a marquee player, and having such a star in New York would provide a tremendous boost for the fledgling league.

Sonny Werblin, a Broadway entrepreneur who was the president of the Jets, had recently put together a television deal for the league, moving it from ABC to NBC for $36 million over a five-year period. Not that the contract was worth much without a showstopper, something Werblin readily recognized.

That centerpiece would be Joe Namath.

In those days, the $100,000 salary barrier was impressive. No athletes in team sports made more. Werblin signed the native of Beaver Falls, Pennsylvania—not far from where such greats as Stan Musial and Ken Griffey in baseball, Joe Montana and Jim Kelly in football grew up—for an astounding $427,000 over three years.

"At the time, it was unheard of," said Namath of his salary. "I was all fired up, excited about playing pro football, coming to New York, all that. Then I got the first paycheck. It was made out to Joseph W. Nathan. Can you imagine that? They didn't even have my name right.

"I got it cashed, though. I had friends in Birmingham."

Soon he would have friends everywhere, particularly throughout the AFL and, of course, in the Big Apple. Werblin, in particular, was a guiding light.

"Over the years," Namath said, "Mr. Werblin adopted me. He made sure I was getting along well. He told me to get to know New York, that it was the greatest city."

The charismatic quarterback listened well. He became a man about town, a true celebrity in a city full of them. Down the road, celebrity would be de rigeur for most athletes, but back then it was something few football players aspired to. High visibility, though, came naturally to Namath.

He modeled pantyhose. He grew a Fu Manchu mustache, then shaved it off for a fee. He wore flowing fur coats and high-heeled boots.

He dated models and actresses. His name could be found in society pages as well as the sports section. He made movies. Namath was pro football's first superstar, someone who transcended the game.

Namath was a flamboyant player, too. He trusted that cannon arm, gambling often by throwing into heavy coverage, believing he could put the ball past or through defenders into the arms of waiting receivers. That led to many big plays: In 1967, he became the first passer to go over 4,000 yards in one season with 4,007 in 14 games.

But it also led to many interceptions.

Plagued by bad knees from his college days, Namath never was the dominant pro quarterback people envisioned he'd be. A surpassing personality, certainly. A perennial All-Pro, hardly.

But he did win the most important football game of modern times, and he did it, naturally, with style.

After two Super Bowls in which the Green Bay Packers of the established NFL routed the AFL representatives, the older league was getting a bit haughty, and there was a threat the title game would lose its luster. For Super Bowl III in January 1969, the oddsmakers helped feed the NFL's confidence by establishing the Baltimore Colts as 17-point favorites.

The Jets scoffed at such odds. Namath went further.

He modeled pantyhose. He grew a Fu Manchu mustache, then shaved it off for a fee. His name could be found in society pages as well as the sports section.

"For two weeks, we were told how we were going to lose," Namath said "When you keep hearing your team isn't going to win, you get angry and frustrated. The anger festers.

"Anger," he adds with a smile, "is a good thing to have."

So Namath stood up at the Miami Touchdown Club dinner during Super Bowl week and said, "We're going to win this game. I GUARANTEE IT."

Except for boxers and professional wrestlers, athletes just didn't do such things. Namath did.

"Coach [Weeb] Ewbank said they would put that up there on the bulletin board and it would give them extra incentive, and I laughed," Namath said. "I said, 'If they need clippings for the bulletin board, they're in trouble.' "

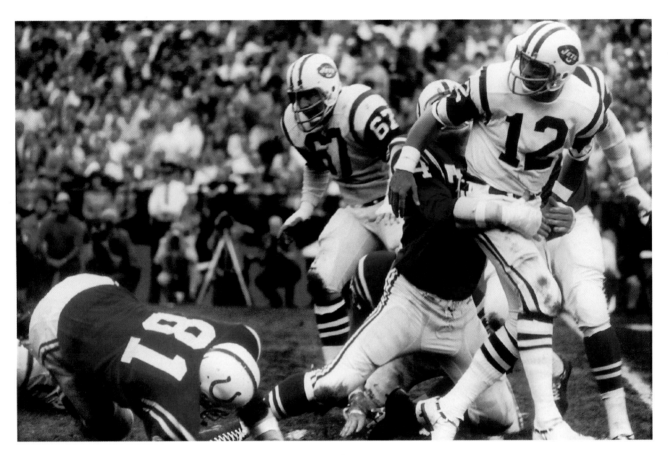

The Colts were unfazed by his prediction. They had been so powerful during the season and playoffs that they considered the Jets a mere annoyance, not a formidable opponent.

"We laughed," said Hall of Fame tight end John Mackey. "We thought it was a joke. That was our problem. We had the wrong attitude. We started to believe we were 17-point favorites. We believed all we had to do was show up. We announced our victory party the Wednesday before the game and cut up the shares at the pre-game meeting. Can you believe that?"

It was exactly what Namath was counting on. Abandoning his swashbuckling style, Namath methodically picked apart the Colts supposedly immovable defense. Never again would he be so precise, but at this critical juncture of his career, Namath became a surgeon.

As his incomparable confidence rubbed off on his teammates, the Colts didn't have a prayer.

"It's got to come from the heart, from deep down," he said. "When I said it, the guarantee, it just came out. It wasn't planned. But we believed it to a man. There wasn't a time when I wished I hadn't said it. It was honest."

By the end of that night, January 12, 1969, Namath was striding off the Orange Bowl field after a shocking 16-7 victory—perhaps the biggest upset in pro sports history—with his index finger wagging in the air. The Jets had a world championship, the AFL had equality, and Namath had lived up to his guarantee.

And, if only for a little while, Namath had taken football out of the gridiron and introduced it to the brilliant lights of Broadway. It was a wild ride no one would forget. The sport, and the men who played it, would never be the same.

Namath had taken football out of the gridiron and introduced it to the brilliant lights of Broadway. It was a wild ride no one would forget.

FLOOD TIDE
Curt Flood

Y ou have a great job, a great salary and great working conditions. You love what you do and you wouldn't change it for the world. You love the city you're in, you have roots.

Suddenly, your boss tells you that you are being transferred to another company, one you don't like. And you have no choice: Transfer, or never work in the same industry again, the industry you trained for all your life. Your world is shattered, but tough luck: it's the law.

Unfair? In 1969, that's exactly what happened to Curt Flood, a center fielder with the St. Louis Cardinals.

Flood was an exceptional baseball player for 12 seasons, winning seven Gold Gloves in an era that featured outfield greats Willie Mays and Roberto Clemente. He played 226 consecutive games without an error at one point, and batted over .300 six times for one of baseball's best teams. The Cardinals won two World Series and three pennants with Flood.

Then they dropped the "T" word on him: Trade. He had been dealt to the Philadelphia Phillies, the worst team in the National League. But Flood stood up to the baseball establishment and said, "I'm not going."

Flood was the first player to challenge baseball's reserve clause that bound players to a team for life without options. And because of this courageous player, the floodgates opened and baseball would never be the same again.

Welcome, free agency.

Like any working person in America, Flood believed he had the right to choose his place of employment.

On December 24, 1969, Flood wrote a letter to baseball commissioner Bowie Kuhn that said, in part: "I do not feel that I am a piece of property to be bought and sold...."

Like any working person in America, Flood believed he had the right to choose his place of employment. Kuhn did not agree. And Flood could have left it there. He was well paid at $90,000, three times the average salary of major leaguers, and the Phillies had offered him a raise. That route would have allowed him to embellish his statistics, inflate his bank account and perhaps help him walk through the doors of the Hall of Fame.

Instead, Flood opened another door.

Many players before him had complained about being traded, but were afraid to challenge the system. Baseball had long perpetuated outdated labor practices, where owners moved players around like chess pieces.

368

For Flood, it wasn't about the money. It was about bucking a system that claimed to uphold American values when it in fact undermined individual freedom and self-determination. Richard Moss, the union's general counsel at the time, said Flood came to him and union head Marvin Miller and told them he wanted to fight the system. "[He said the system] treated people like they were pieces of property."

On January 16, 1970, shortly before his 32nd birthday, Flood filed a $4.1 million-dollar lawsuit against baseball. His charge: The sport had violated antitrust laws by not allowing him freedom of choice in the workplace.

Even though Miller and the Major League Baseball Players Association supported Flood, many players and some segments of the media were not in his corner. The players figured that the end of the reserve clause would mean the end of baseball. Flood was regarded as a rebel who had stepped over the line. He received hate mail from fans, some threatening his life. He was reviled by baseball management. A pariah in his sport. An ingrate.

Flood stood alone.

Flood was an exceptional baseball player for 12 seasons, winning seven Gold Gloves. . .

The Cardinals won two world series and three pennants with Flood. Then they dropped the "T" word on him.

Cardinals catcher Tim McCarver, who was also involved in the trade of seven players, was expected to join the Phillies. He had no thoughts at the time of joining Flood in his crusade, and recalled few players at the time who wanted to stick their necks out. "Players were afraid for their jobs," McCarver said. "I had no designs on being a pioneer."

Flood wasn't exactly what anyone would call an agitator. A Texas native who was the first full-time black player on the Cardinals, he was a quiet, introspective person and one of the best liked on the team. "More than any player, whether he went 3-for-4 or 0-for-4, he would root for the other guys," McCarver said. "That stood out in bold caps." New York Yankees manager Joe Torre regarded his former teammate as "someone with great depth."

But Flood was also someone with great passion for a cause, and would refer to himself later as "a child of the sixties," someone who grew up in an era of revolutionary social change. For him, there was something greater at stake than just baseball. He didn't give up when both the District Court and Court of Appeals ruled in favor of baseball. He took his fight to the Supreme Court, with union chief Miller as his ally. Former Supreme Court Justice Arthur Goldberg accepted Flood's case, agreeing to work for expenses.

As he waited for his case to be resolved by the nation's highest court, Flood sat

out the 1970 season. He missed baseball—so much so that he agreed to play for the Washington Senators once he was assured that it would not jeopardize his lawsuit. The Senators had worked out a deal to obtain the rights to Flood, who was happy just to be back in the game.

Others were apparently not of the same mind. Pitcher Bob Gibson, a friend of Flood's, wrote that when Flood returned to his locker one day, he found a funeral wreath on it. Flood's season was nearly as depressing. He struggled for 13 games before quitting.

"I tried," Flood said in a telegram to Senators owner Robert Short. "A year and a half [away from the game] is too much. Very serious problems mounting …" He left America for Spain and never played major-league baseball again.

On June 19, 1972, the Supreme Court decision finally came down, ruling 5-3 against Flood's suit. The baseball owners had won.

Or had they?

In writing his decision upholding the reserve clause, Justice Harry Blackmun said the Supreme Court didn't think it was its place to make such a decision. It was Congress' job to change the law, he said. "[The reserve clause is] an aberration that has been with us for half a century,"

Finally, in 1975, an arbitrator struck down the infamous reserve clause and pitchers Andy Messersmith and Dave McNally were granted free agency. Players, not owners, were now free to decide their fate. Even though Flood lost his personal battle, he eventually won the war.

The revolutionary process was under way, and not only in baseball. Free agency, a phrase created by Flood, became a part of the American sports lexicon. Athletes were now able to select where they wanted to play and to set up competition for their services, resulting in escalating salaries.

Shaquille O'Neal signed a hard-to-believe $120 million contract with the Los Angeles Lakers, the richest in basketball until Kevin Garnett signed a $125 million deal with the Minnesota Timberwolves…. Kevin Brown became the first $100 million player in baseball when he joined the Los Angeles Dodgers … football star Chad Brown received a $24 million payoff from the Seattle Seahawks … and Sergei Fedorov picked up a cool $28 million for playing about three and a half months of hockey after a long holdout and contract battle with the Detroit Red Wings. O'Neal, the two Browns, and Fedorov were only a few examples of free agents in the four major sports who benefited from Flood's courageous battle.

"So much of what you have," manager Torre once told his New York Yankees, "is because of this man."

In 1998, President Clinton signed the "Curt Flood Act." It overrode a long-standing Supreme Court law which exempted baseball from antitrust laws on the basis that it was not interstate commerce.

"[Flood's] enormous talents on the baseball diamond were matched by his courage off the field," Clinton said. "His bold stand set in motion the events that culminated in the bill I have signed into law."

Flood, who died in 1997, did not see himself in such a noble and extravagant light. Once asked to describe his legacy, he replied simply:

"Just a ballplayer who tried to do what was right."

The revolutionary process was under way, and not only in baseball. Free agency, a phrase created by Flood, became a part of the American sports lexicon.

KING OF THE ROAD
Richard Petty

You are a normal American male. As you sit behind the wheel of your Ford or Toyota or whatever you're driving, a natural instinct overcomes you. What would it be like to push down on the accelerator a little harder than usual?

And keep pushing. And pushing—right down to the floor.

What would it be like to rocket your way down the road as if you were at Daytona or Talladega or Indianapolis? What would it be like to be Richard Petty? The guy in the STP uniform driving the No. 43 car to victory after victory, who's carried stock car racing with him out of the boondocks and back roads and into the American sporting mainstream?

What would it be like to be "the King"?

Well, for one thing, you would have begun your career before there were any organized races. As Petty described it, "I started when there were four or five thousand people in the grandstands at a lot of the tracks we ran. Things have changed a bit."

A bit. Stock car racing at the end of the 20th century was the fastest-growing sport in America. Its television ratings at times rivaled those of NFL regular-season games, the measuring stick in TV sports.

"He is one of the key players," says Bill France, Jr., who along with his late father, Bill, Sr. started NASCAR. "If you started listing a handful, his name

"Certainly the most important thing was he took more time signing autographs for fans than any other athlete in America," France says. "Year-in and year-out, race-in and race-out, he thought about what was good for auto racing."

would be right there. He was a great ambassador for the sport as a racer, and he still is after his career ended."

Petty came by his driving skills naturally. His father, Lee, was one of NASCAR's pioneers, a man who built his own cars and engines and, in the days before organized events, would "go racin'" against all comers, mostly in North Carolina. His crew in the early days of the official stock-car circuit consisted of Richard and younger brother Maurice.

"In 1949, when Bill France, Sr., was getting NASCAR started, I was 11 years old and my daddy took me to the very first of those races, at Charlotte," Richard recalled. "It was a 200-lap race and he had this '46 Buick Roadmaster. Didn't run too well that day, though."

Back home in Level Cross, North Carolina, Richard and Maurice would attend school, then head for the family garage to help Lee put together a race car capable of running with the likes of Red Byron, Bill Rexford, Tim Flock, Herb Thomas and the other groundbreakers of stock-car racing.

By the time he was 14, Richard was his father's crew chief, which meant traveling throughout the South, soaking up the intricacies of a sport in which, no matter how talented the driver is, "he ain't goin' nowhere without a good race car."

So the Pettys learned how to put together good race cars, and Lee would win three driving championships. In 1958, as his father was taking his second of those titles, Richard was driving in the top NASCAR series, too.

By 1959, he was the rookie of the year, and in 1960, he began compiling the most incredible racing resume ever: 200 victories; seven driving titles; 158 runner-up finishes; seasons of 27, 21, 18 and 16 victories; 1,177 starts; 126 poles.

And one All-American legend.

"If you go back and look at all the billions of people that have been born, I was born in the right place, at the right time, to the right people and under the right circumstances, for me," Petty said.

Part of Petty's appeal stemmed from his early deal with Plymouth. He fully understood the importance of the relationship between automaker and driver. Petty not only benefited from the loyalty of everyday drivers to their car manufacturer, but the bitterness fans felt toward other carmakers: a true, deeply imbedded rivalry existed in those days between Chevy owners and Ford owners.

"When the Ford man fell out, those people weren't about to pull for a Chevrolet," he said. "But they'd pull for someone in a Plymouth to beat that Chevrolet. And vice versa.

"Then I think they finally said, 'The heck with this,' and hung in the middle. I was always in neutral ground."

But that wouldn't entirely explain Petty's eventual celebrity. As NASCAR began making inroads on all levels, expanding its top circuit to California, Pennsylvania, Michigan and other areas hardly known as good ol' boy territory, Petty was the point man. That didn't just mean running at the point in races, but being accessible, sociable, and downright lovable away from the track.

Petty's popularity throughout the South was so overwhelming that when he held an autograph session at his family home in 1967, it drew 12,000 people. He signed for eight hours.

When Petty again held an open house in 1992, nearly 65,000 fans showed up, forming a line that stretched three miles. Some came from as far away as New England and Texas, looking to catch a glimpse of the King.

"When the Ford man fell out, those people weren't about to pull for a Chevrolet. But they'd pull for someone in a Plymouth to beat the Chevrolet."

In 1965, Petty quit driving in NASCAR races when Chrysler pulled out because of a dispute over engines. Rather than switch brands or use his considerable influence—he'd already won 36 races—Petty chose to drive in exhibitions at backwater tracks from Florida to Virginia.

That rebellious streak certainly touched the fans, many of whom got the opportunity to see Petty drive at the local dirt track, then meet him as he chatted and signed autographs.

"Certainly the most important thing was he took more time signing autographs for fans than any other athlete in America," France says. "Year-in and year-out, race-in and race-out, he thought about what was good for auto racing."

But mostly he enjoyed his fans. "There were some fun times, just meeting with the folks and talking about racing, person-to-person and stuff," Petty said. "It's always been important to me to connect with the fans and for them to feel something special for our sport and our race team. It's something I've tried to do no matter where I'm racing or making appearances. They're entitled to it, because of the support they've given us."

That support could easily have wavered in 1967. Stock-car racing was suffering from warring factions and the burgeoning prominence of pro football, basketball and golf; furthermore, it was losing its star players: Lee Petty had retired. So had Ned Jarrett and Junior Johnson. Fireball Roberts had died from injuries suffered in a crash at Charlotte.

Petty quickly moved into place, taking care of any concerns about where the new star would come from with the most dominant season in motor sports history. Perhaps in all of sports history. In no year was Petty more regal—or more important—than '67.

He won 10 races in a row (albeit some of the victories were against lesser competition at short tracks off the beaten path—but still sanctioned by NASCAR). He entered 48 races, unimaginable by today's standards, where drivers and crews feel stretched to the limit to handle 34. He won 27.

Twenty-seven!

He did it with style. Petty won from in front and with gut-wrenching rallies. He got to the checkered flag first by squeezing between rivals, or running inside of them when they looked high, or outside when they bet he would go low.

Perhaps most significantly, he

"It's always been important to me to connect with the fans and for them to feel something special for our sport and our race team."

He got to the checkered flag first by squeezing between rivals, or running inside of them when they looked high, or outside when they bet he would go low.

won over countless fans. Not just Carolinians and Georgians, but Californians and Texans, New Yorkers and Ohioans.

Even Canadians.

"I got a clipping out of a paper from somewhere in Canada about this big," he said, holding his fingers several inches apart. "The headline was: 'PETTY RUNS SECOND.' And the little story tells, wherever we ran—Spartanburg or somewhere—about Richard Petty. It doesn't even tell who won the race."

The King indeed.

Still, for all his pull with the public and his engaging personality, Petty needed some help in carrying stock-car racing into the full American sporting consciousness. He got it thanks to other Hall of Fame drivers such as David Pearson, with whom Petty had a fierce rivalry, Bobby Allison and Cale Yarborough.

Many of the Petty-Pearson hookups were classics, and both held a healthy respect for the other.

"I didn't mind losing to David so much, because I knew he was one great race-car driver," Petty said.

"The thing about Richard," Pearson recalled, "is he would go all out to beat you in any race, at Daytona or Charlotte, or on a dirt track on a Saturday night. I felt the same way, and it made for some great racing."

And great memories—none more special than the 1976 Daytona 500, which many race fans say had the greatest finish the sport has seen.

By then, Petty's star had risen far out of the NASCAR galaxy. Just as Arnold Palmer or Billie Jean King or Muhammad Ali had transcended their sport and become national icons, so had Petty. Pearson, hardly as affable or smooth with the public and media, never would be a megastar of Petty's magnitude. But on the track, he usually was Petty's equal.

For most of those 500 miles, Petty and Pearson raced in tandem. Heading into the final lap, Petty led, with Pearson on his bumper. These were the years before engine speed was restricted, and the second-place car had an advantage—it could pull out and slingshot past the leader thanks to the aerodynamic push created by the car in front.

Pearson pulled out entering the third of the four turns at Daytona, but Petty then cut inside and pulled in front as they went into the final turn, just a few hundred yards from the finish.

"That's when I made a mistake," said Petty, who to this day says the '76 500 will be the race for which he is remembered, even though he lost. "I drifted into his left side and we both went into the wall."

Pearson managed to keep his engine going, despite crashing, while Petty stalled out and drifted into the grass infield. As he sat in the STP 43, he saw Pearson chug to the finish line, going about 10 mph, to take the checkered flag.

"Damndest finish I ever seen," Petty said.

As he sat in the STP 43, he saw Pearson chug to the finish line, going about 10 mph, to take the checkered flag.

Petty, of course, wasn't even close to finished. In fact, he beat Pearson the next week at Rockingham, and headed toward the unimaginable 200-win barrier.

Along the way, Petty remained the people's choice, his popularity growing. The small-town kid from North Carolina knew just how to build his image. He became an advertising wonder, endorsing dozens of products in the days when athletes were just becoming bigtime hawksters. From auto parts to food, Petty was the man advertisers pursued to cash in on the exploding car racing market.

He also dived deeply into the memorabilia and paraphernalia game. Today, at any NASCAR race, dozens of trailers sell both

From auto parts to food, Petty was the man advertisers pursued to cash in on the exploding car racing market.

cheap and pricey souvenirs for just about every driver on the circuit. It's a billion-dollar business, and it all started with Petty's people setting up stands to sell T-shirts and mementos.

Petty—who owns the No. 43 car currently driven by John Andretti—is now the patriarch of a family that includes his son Kyle, a Winston Cup veteran driver, and grandson Adam, who drives in NASCAR's second level Busch Grand National series. Petty marvels at how the sport has grown financially. He means the increase in NASCAR purses and the willingness of fans to open their own.

"The monetary deal is something you can't gauge anything off of," Petty said. "In 1959 my father won as many races as anybody. He won the championship. He won Daytona and wound up with $54,000 or something like that for the whole year.

"But it's all relative. Back then we were making as much money as anybody else, whether it was $100 or $1,000. I drove 15 years and won everything there was to win before I won a million dollars. Now if you hit the right two or three races you can win a million bucks. They've got people on the circuit who have won more money than I have and never won a race. We won 200 of them."

No. 200, which was voted the greatest moment in NASCAR history in a 1996 fan ballot, climaxed Petty's 1984 season. Although he would drive until his 1992 farewell tour (which overshadowed that year's races), the Independence Day victory at Daytona was his last win.

That charge to the finish came before an audience of 80,000 that included

President Reagan, in the midst of his re-election campaign. Reagan, still aboard Air Force One on his way to the track, gave the instructions to start the race from the airplane.

But he made it on time to see his fellow Republican—Petty would lose an election for North Carolina secretary of state in 1996—edge Yarborough by a fender under a yellow flag with three laps to go. Yarborough, incidentally, was a staunch Democrat, and he was so befuddled by the proceedings that he pulled into the pits one lap too early under the caution, winding up third.

Oddly, Petty won just over $43,000 for his 200th win. Not that the money mattered. It rarely does for superstars.

"It wasn't a deal where I set out to do it," Petty said. "I think that's what made it natural. It was just me. It was my personality.

"If nobody had drawn attention to it I probably wouldn't have thought anything about it."

Long live the King.

INSPIRATION MAN
Knute Rockne

A master motivator, the Notre Dame football coach could wrench tears from his strapping athletes and sometimes get them so angry they flattened everything in their rush to get out to the field.

It was just before the Notre Dame-Army football game of 1928 and Knute Rockne really needed to come up with an inspirational locker-room talk. His Notre Dame team was a huge underdog to the undefeated Cadets, and it looked like the Fighting Irish might be in for a bad day.

Unless Knute could think of something to turn the tide.

His players always wondered what Rockne was going to say before a game. A master motivator, the Notre Dame football coach could wrench tears from his strapping athletes and sometimes get them so angry they flattened everything in their rush to get out to the field.

This time, Rockne had hit on an idea that couldn't lose: George Gipp. The one-time Notre Dame football star and bad boy had died prematurely of a strep throat infection eight years before, and now Rockne was going to raise him up just like Lazarus. He soon had the team's undivided attention with a compelling story about visiting Gipp in the hospital. According to Rockne, the dying player whispered a special request:

"… Sometime, Rock, when the team is up against it, when things are going wrong and the breaks are beating the boys—tell them to go in there with all they've got and win just one for the Gipper. I don't know where I'll be then, Rock. But I'll know about it, and I'll be happy."

Why Rockne had waited so many years to pull the speech out of his hat, no one seemed to care. The galvanized Notre Dame football players practically beat down the doors and each other getting out to the field at Yankee Stadium that day. Then they beat Army 12-6, adding another chapter to the growing Rockne legend.

The "Win one for the Gipper" speech became the most famous and most quoted locker-room talk in American sports history, later glorified in the movie *Knute Rockne, All-American*. Even today, a "Rockne speech" is a synonym for an inspirational talk. And while there are believers and there are skeptics about Gipp's final plea, there is no doubting that Rockne had a creative flair for telling a story and a genius for preparing players for the game. And for winning them.

In 13 years at Notre Dame, Rockne's teams only lost 12 times—incredible when you consider that many of the Irish's big games against national powers, particularly early in Rockne's coaching career, were played on the road. Rockne was trying to build a reputation for his tiny Catholic school in Indiana, and what better way to do it than traveling all over the country and challenging all comers? Especially if your team usually won.

Rockne's winning percentage of .881 was remarkable enough. But not only did he put Notre Dame on the football map, he raised the popularity of the sport with an exciting,

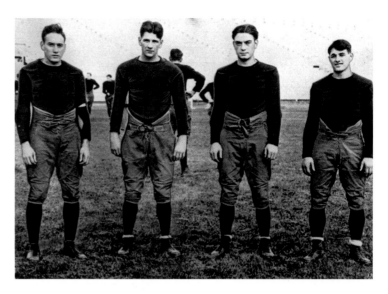

wide-open style that featured long passes and long, game-breaking runs. For the most part, football had been pure brute force in those days. Rockne showed that the little guy could win with smart, heads-up play by using speed and deception.

The innovative "Notre Dame Shift" was formidable. All four backs moved in unison before the snap of the ball, choreographed like a chorus line. The often-baffled opposition hated it, the fans loved it. Rockne was making the sport more attractive to fans and fun to watch, captivating an entire nation. With his wide-open attack, Rockne brought football into the modern age, and along with him came Notre Dame heroes that were forever blistered in the American consciousness. Like the Four Horsemen of the Apocalypse, for instance (better known as Stuhldreher, Miller, Crowley, and Layden). And of course, the Gipper.

Along with creating heroes that fans could identify with, Rockne built himself into a superstar among coaches with his theatrical flair and impishness. The hard-working Rockne had become a national hero as big as Babe Ruth. Meanwhile, he put his brain to work improving everything he could in the game.

He designed his own equipment and uniforms, reducing the bulk and weight of the equipment while increasing its protectiveness and introducing materials for uniforms that cut down on wind resistance. And in addition to "the shift," there were other tactical improvements as well. In a day of one-platoon football, Rockne featured specialists in his offense. Notre Dame's "Shock Troops" was another Rockne innovation. He would start the second-stringers, usually rough players who gave the opposing team a pretty good physical pounding. Then came the first-stringers, after their opponents had been physically abused to further demoralize them.

And although Rockne didn't invent the forward pass, he did exploit it and help bring it to a new level: it made the Notre Dame attack the most exciting in football.

Born in Voss, Norway, Rockne had come to America in 1893 with his family and settled in Chicago.

Rockne brought football into the modern age, and along with him came Notre Dame heroes . . . like the Four Horsemen of the Apocalypse (better known as Stuhldreher, Miller, Crowley, and Layden).

Still, the boys from West Point needed an opponent—any opponent—and Notre Dame would suffice.

As a child, Rockne had played football on sandlots with his neighbors, and he took up the game in high school, along with pole-vaulting and sprinting. He was expelled after cutting classes to practice for a track meet, but it did not keep him from furthering his education. He worked for three years to save up to go to college. He decided on Notre Dame because he felt his money could go farther there and thought he could find work easily in South Bend, Indiana. Because he didn't have a high school diploma, he had to pass an entrance exam first. No problem.

He was the quintessential student athlete, excellent at both sports and studies. At Notre Dame, Rockne set a school record in the indoor pole vault, and when he tried out for football, he eventually made third-string end.

And then he made captain of the team. It was 1913, a year that would stand out as not only the turning point in his life but the turning point for the game of football as well. After one fateful game against the Army football team at West Point, everything would change.

Army had needed someone to play after Yale had backed out of their scheduled game on November 1. The Cadets' football manager looked through the Spalding Football Guide and found a small school in Indiana that had gone unbeaten in two previous seasons, outscoring opponents 611-36 in 15 games. The statistics were remarkable, indeed, but who had ever heard of Notre Dame? At the time, the seat of football power in the country was in the East, and Army was one of the top teams.

Still, the boys from West Point needed an opponent—any opponent—and

Notre Dame would suffice. If nothing else, the Cadets figured they could get a good workout tuning up for the rest of the season against more formidable opponents. The Cadets had every right to feel smug: They outweighed the Notre Dame team 15 pounds to the man.

So the military academy paid Notre Dame $1,000 to come to West Point for a game. It still wasn't enough to guarantee the poor Notre Dame players the proper equipment. They were only able to round up 14 pairs of cleats for the 18 players. Most of them had dual-purpose shoes and stuck the cleats on them only if they were required to play. The supplies for their trip were equally spartan—the school refectory prepared sandwiches and fruit for the players' arduous two-day train trip to West Point. The entire Notre Dame campus turned out to see them off.

"The morning we left South Bend, every student and professor was out of bed long before breakfast and marched downtown accompanying the team to the railroad station," remembered Rockne. "It was the first time I'd seen anything like this mass hysteria generated on the Notre Dame campus over a football game, and it made every one of the players so excited, they wanted to march on to West Point."

The Fighting Irish had more than just motivation going for them as they boarded the train for the trip east. They had confidence. Particularly Rockne and Gus Dorais, the team quarterback. Despite the odds against their team, the pair had every expectation of surprising the football world. The Fighting Irish were going to spring a "secret weapon" on the high and mighty Cadets.

At the suggestion of coach Jesse Harper, Rockne and Dorais had spent the summer before throwing the football around. They weren't just playing catch—

"It was the first time I'd seen anything like this mass hysteria generated on the Notre Dame campus over a football game, and it made every one of the players so excited, they wanted to march on to West Point."

they hoped to install a passing attack into the Notre Dame offense in the 1913 season, and practiced their techniques at a beach resort in Cedar Point, Ohio. "I'd run along the beach, Dorais would throw from all angles," Rockne said. "People who didn't know [that] we were two college seniors making painstaking preparations for our final season probably thought we were crazy."

The use of the pass had been practically foreign to football in those days, mostly because a dropped pass was considered a fumble and the ball was fair game for both teams. The size of the football did not lend itself to passing, either. It was larger and more rounded than it is today. A football player needed hands of extraordinary size to throw it. Dorais was only 5-foot-7 and weighed 145 pounds, but … he had huge hands.

Army, expecting an easy game, got the unexpected when Dorais started unleashing his passes. As the Army defense piled toward the center of the line to stop the predictable bucks and plunges, Dorais completed an 11-yard pass for a first down.

"It was amusing to see the Army boys huddle [after the first pass completion]," Rockne remembered.

You can imagine how the "Army boys" felt when Dorais went deep to Rockne a couple of plays later. In the huddle, Dorais called Rockne's number, meaning he was going to throw him a long pass as he ran down the field and out toward the sideline. Rockne had been slammed hard on an earlier play. But always the actor, he pretended he was hurt and started limping down the field as the play unfolded.

"The Army halfback covering me almost yawned in my face, he was that bored…." Rockne said.

Suddenly, Rockne put on a burst of speed and left his opponent frozen in his tracks. Rockne raced across the Army goal line with Dorais' pass settling in his hands, completing a 40-yard pass.

"Everybody seemed astonished," Rockne said. "There had been no hurdling, no tackling, no plunging, no crushing of fiber and sinew. Just a long distance touchdown by rapid transit."

Notre Dame crushed Army 35-13, and football was never the same.

If Rockne had done nothing else but play in that 1913 Notre Dame-Army game, his place in college football history would be secure. But his later coaching success placed him among such greats as Amos Alonzo Stagg in college and George Halas in the pros, who also helped to reshape the sport into the game we know today. Stagg's technical contributions in nearly 60 years of coaching were especially impressive, but few coaches were in Rockne's league to help popularize the game.

Following his championship season in 1931, Rockne was scheduled to make a football demonstration movie in Los Angeles. He boarded a plane in Kansas City that flew into a storm and crashed into a wheat field shortly after takeoff. He was 43. Twenty years later, Rockne was named the top college football coach of all time by the Associated Press.

THE COWBOY AND THE KING
Tex Rickard and Don King

In one brilliant stroke, Rickard had taken boxing from the Ice Age to a New Age.

It was the wild, wild west and a gambling man was about to change the face of boxing. The time was the early 1900s, the place was the small mining town of Goldfield, Nevada, and the gambler was Tex Rickard. He was about to gain or lose a fortune.

Rickard should have been scared. He didn't know much about boxing and had no connections in the game. but he knew a thing or two about gambling, having spent seven years in Alaska's gambling dens to the tune of $65,000. It was likely the idea of similar gains that motivated Rickard and other Goldfield citizens to back a championship bout between lightweight titleholder Joe Gans and challenger Oscar "Battling" Nelson. It was probably Rickard's idea to guarantee the fighters an astounding $30,000 purse. In that day, there were no guaranteed purses, and certainly not the small fortune that Rickard had promised the fighters.

According to Rickard's autobiography, *Memoirs of a Master Promoter*, this initial foray into boxing happened quite by accident. While reading a newspaper, he saw an article about a fight between Gans and Nelson. Everything was set, except a place to hold it.

"Up to that moment my eye fell on that item, I had never so much as thought of even seeing a prize fight—a big one, I mean," Rickard said. "On the spur of

the moment, I threw the paper aside, walked over to the telegraph office and sent a message to [Bill] Nolan, the manager of Battling Nelson."

Rickard asked Nolan how much he would want to hold the Gans-Nelson fight in Goldfield. Upon receiving the reply, Rickard ran around town with the telegram in his hands drumming up contributions. Within an hour, he had his $30,000 guarantee.

Rickard stacked the entire amount in gold pieces in the window of a bank, stating it was the purse for the fighters. That picture was worth thousands of words in newspapers across the country.

Goldfield residents had never seen the

He joined forces with Jack Dempsey, and their partnership resulted in boxing's first million-dollar gate.

type of crowds lured by Rickard's main event, nor would they ever again. But the ones lucky enough to snare a ticket for the bout on September 3, 1906 did get their money's worth. Gans and Nelson battled through 41 ferocious rounds. Finally, in the 42nd the champion was sent to the canvas when Nelson hit him with a shot to the groin. Gans was declared the winner on the foul.

The aptly named Goldfield turned out to be a gold mine for Rickard, who walked away with nearly $14,000 tax-free and a reputation as a major boxing promoter. The event also was a watershed for boxing. Many state governments relaxed their anti-boxing laws when they realized how much money could be made from the sport. By the 1920s, boxing's legitimacy had been established once and for all.

With the Gans-Nelson fight, George Lewis "Tex" Rickard transformed boxing from a sport to a business. In one brilliant stroke, Rickard had taken boxing from the Ice Age to a New Age.

Rickard had arrived on the boxing scene with a bang. In his autobiography, he claims to have entered the world the same way. Born in a roadside cabin in Clay County, Missouri, on January 2, 1871, with a hail of bullets flying nearby, Rickard recalled that the bullets were meant for outlaw Jesse James, whose mother lived down the road, and who was being pursued by law enforcement officers.

Rickard pretty much lived his life at the same pace. Before promoting fights, Rickard had been successively a cowboy, a town marshal in Texas, a prospector in the Yukon, a gambling-saloon owner in the Klondike and Nevada gold rushes, a soldier of fortune in South Africa and a cattle baron in Paraguay. Rickard made and lost fortunes along the way in exotic locales around the world, but it wasn't until he settled in New York City that his greatest adventure began.

He joined forces with Jack Dempsey, and their partnership resulted in boxing's first million-dollar gate. About the same time, Rickard also was making his presence felt on the New York sports scene.

Rickard had promoted a heavyweight championship fight between Dempsey and Jess Willard in Toledo, Ohio, in 1919. He found a meal ticket in Dempsey, who ripped the heavyweight title away from the giant Willard.

Rickard was at his promotional best when he later set up a fight between Dempsey and Georges Carpentier in 1921. Rickard knew that Carpentier, a popular but undersized heavyweight from France, realistically didn't stand a chance against Dempsey, and Rickard couldn't sell the fight on its competitive merits alone. As he had done so often in the past, he used symbolism instead—in this case, a hero (Carpentier) versus a villain (Dempsey).

The handsome Carpentier was a decorated national war hero in France. Dempsey, the beetle-browed "Manassa Mauler," was disparaged as a "slacker" for having stayed out of the First World War. The contest developed into a fight for ideals, and Rickard encouraged the theme.

It was no surprise to boxing insiders when Dempsey knocked out Carpentier in the fourth round of the bout in Jersey City. It was also a victory for Rickard.

It didn't matter to Rickard whether any of his fighters were evenly matched. He wanted his audience to cheer the hero and hiss the villain.

He had the biggest crowd (90,000) and the biggest gate ($1.7 million) in boxing history at that point.

It didn't matter to Rickard whether any of his fighters were evenly matched. He wanted his audience to cheer the hero and hiss the villain. To Rickard, it was all black and white—literally. He knew opposites attracted and had used the strategy when he staged a fight earlier in his career between black champion Jack Johnson and white challenger Jim Jeffries.

Johnson won handily over the out-of-condition Jeffries. Jeffries had been called out of retirement to fight the "white" cause against the black champion. When Jeffries was defeated, it sparked race riots around the country. Rickard had done his job all too well, but was distressed at the racial unrest.

The so-called Golden Age of Sport, the 1920s, was just that for Rickard. He designed a series of big-money fights featuring Dempsey, topped by the $2.7 million gate in his 1927 battle with Gene Tunney. In nine fights starting with the bout against Willard in 1919, 576,213 people paid more than $9.2 million to see Dempsey fight under Rickard's hand. The numbers were astounding for the time, considering there was no television.

However, it was not nearly as satisfying to Rickard as one special night in New York in 1925.

The city was going to lose a landmark—Madison Square Garden, a sports arena that Rickard was managing and which, for the first time, was profitable. When news came that the outmoded Garden would be razed, Rickard suggested a site farther uptown for a new sports palace, this one on Eighth Avenue between 49th and 50th streets. With the aid of circus magnate John Ringling and Wall Street backers, a new Madison Square Garden was built. It didn't matter that it wasn't on Madison Square. Rickard wanted to retain the famous name, and the new Garden opened to rave reviews on December 15, 1925.

When the crowds started pouring into the Garden, Rickard could usually be seen there twirling his trademark gold-headed cane, wearing a straw topper, a smile on his face while smoking a cigar. He was happy "seeing the evening dress, the ladies, the big people out there." He was especially proud that he was now drawing a female audience to his fights. They felt safe being shown to their reserved seats by ushers, their safety guaranteed by guards. Ringside seats, a novel concept at the time, had inspired public trust.

Rickard died prematurely of appendicitis with an emotional Dempsey at his side in 1929. "His word was better than a gold bond," Dempsey said. "He never went back on it." Rickard lay in state in the new Madison Square Garden, the so-called "House That Tex Built." His friends from the press were there. As usual, a newspaperman had the last word.

"It doesn't matter whether Tex goes to heaven or hell," he said. "He'll probably wind up promoting a match with the other side, anyway."

Billing himself as "The World's Greatest Promoter," King has created a circuslike atmosphere around his fights and found creative ways to make fantastic sums of money.

A black P.T. Barnum in a tuxedo, glittering with gold and diamonds, the mountainous Don King enters the ring when the final bell has rung. His champion fighter has just knocked out another opponent, and the body is hardly cold on the canvas before King is already promoting his next fight.

A supreme showman, King arrived on the boxing scene in full force in the 1970s. He was an aggressive numbers runner in Cleveland who went to jail for killing a man and, remarkably, emerged from prison to become the most influential boxing promoter in the latter part of the twentieth century.

Billing himself as "The World's Greatest Promoter," King has created a circuslike atmosphere around his fights and found creative ways to make fantastic sums of money. Like Rickard, King had the extraordinary sense to recognize the public's needs and fulfill them.

Growing up in Cleveland, King was always a hustler. He made money delivering live chickens to a slaughter house and sold peanuts and pies made by his family to gambling houses. As a teenager, King thought about becoming a lawyer. But when he saw how much money he could make as a numbers runner, King started working for his brother—and before long, his brother was working for him. King had become one of the leading numbers racketeers in Cleveland and prided himself on being "a respected man in the community because I always paid off."

Apparently, not everyone was happy with the way King conducted business. He remembered making some enemies "who came after me with machine guns. Wanted to blow my house down, kidnap my kids." King was lucky to escape one attack in 1957, when his front porch was destroyed.

Living on the edge was precarious, and King did finally end up in jail, when he killed a man in an argument over a $600

A man of the streets, King found that another kind of violence was safer—in the boxing ring.

gambling debt. In a previous case, King had been acquitted in a shooting death of another man when the court ruled justifiable homicide. This time, he was sent to the Marion (Ohio) Correctional Institution. He stayed there for nearly four years and called it "one of my alma maters." In a sense, it was. While in jail, King studied the classics and Shakespeare. Later, he constantly quoted the Bard and other classic writers while hyping his fights.

A man of the streets, King found that another kind of violence was safer—in the boxing ring.

It all started with an invitation. In 1972, King asked Muhammad Ali to stage an exhibition fight in Cleveland. The all-black Forest City Hospital, which served the poor and working-class community, was in danger of going under. Ali accepted, helped raise $82,500 to save the hospital, and their relationship was cemented.

The next time King asked Ali to fight for him, the stakes were considerably higher. It was two years later and the fight was a long way from Cleveland. This time, King didn't have to sell Ali on the fight with George Foreman. He was going to guarantee each fighter the unheard-of sum of $5 million.

But where was he going to get the money? Now he brought his well-known persuasive talents to a third-world country. All King had to do was convince the president of Zaire, Mobutu Sese Seko, to finance the fight. Mobutu enthusiastically accepted the idea, and the "Rumble in the Jungle" made history on October 30, 1974. It was a knockout success as Ali recaptured his heavyweight title with an eighth-round KO, Zaire grabbed worldwide attention, and King established himself as a champion promoter. Just as Rickard had made his name with the Gans-Nelson fight in Goldfield, so King established his reputation as a big-time promoter with the Ali-Foreman battle in Zaire.

King continued to raise the stakes, with the help of cable and pay-per-view TV. Before long, the $5 million paid to Ali and Foreman in the "Rumble" fight seemed like a mere pittance—King was the first promoter, in 1981, to guarantee $1 million to non-heavyweights, and that same year, he was the first promoter to guarantee a $10 million purse, to Sugar Ray Leonard.

In the final three decades of the century, it was hard to find an important fight where King wasn't involved. He struck a blow for black entrepreneurs in a field that had previously been dominated by whites.

From 1978 to 1990, King basically controlled the heavyweight title with Larry Holmes and Mike Tyson as his clients. In 1982 and 1983 alone, King staged a staggering 34 championship bouts in different weight classes. His clients included the biggest names in boxing: Ali, Foreman, Leonard, Mike Tyson, Larry Holmes, Ken Norton, Roberto Duran, and Julio Cesar Chavez among them.

Love him or hate him—and he has inspired plenty of both emotions—King's globe-trotting productions resulted in some of the most exciting boxing bouts in history: Ali-Foreman in Zaire, Tyson-Buster Douglas in Tokyo, Holmes-Norton in Las Vegas, Ali-Joe Frazier in Manila.

The Tyson-Evander Holyfield fight in Las Vegas in 1996 topped them all, at least in terms of money. The gross by most estimates: $100 million, the first time a bout had reached that euphoric level.

King's stormy, symbiotic relationship with Tyson featured two of the most vilified personalities in sports. It did not hurt their earning power. Tyson's pay-day alone for his second fight with Holyfield was not only memorable for Iron Mike's infamous ear-bite, but for his bite of the take: $30 million.

Meeting King might be described as a hair-raising experience: King's crowning

Love him or hate him—and he has inspired plenty of both emotions—King's globe-trotting productions resulted in some of the most exciting boxing bouts in history.

touch is his famous electric-shock hairdo. King has a unique view of his stand-up hair: "I see my hair, a burning bush basted in righteous juices. . . . For now, my hair has mastered the universe! When I gaze into the mirror, I never cease to amaze myself. And I say this humbly." His "burning bush" is just one more way in which King has made himself a memorable, if not universal, figure in the sports world.

Inducted into the Boxing Hall of Fame in 1997, King was also named one of *Sports Illustrated's* "40 Most Influential Sports Figures of the Past 40 Years."

He's also continued to give back to the community—through the Don King Foundation, through his holiday "Turkey Tours" where he hands out turkeys to needy families, and through frequent donations to organizations such as the NAACP, the Martin Luther King, Jr., Foundation, the Simon Weisenthal Center and many charity organizations. He has received countless awards, among them the NAACP's highest honor, the President's Award, as well as the Martin Luther King, Jr., Humanitarian Award. The IBF, WBA and WBC have proclaimed him the "Greatest Promoter in History."

Not all King's celebrity has been favorable, however. He has also been investigated by law enforcement groups, criticized by the media, and embroiled in controversy with many of his fighters. Lawsuits over contractual agreements and allegations of missing money have made him as compelling as a soap opera star. King's dealings with Tyson ended when the fighter filed a suit accusing the promoter of cheating him out of millions of dollars. When not in a boxing arena, it seems that King has usually been in a courtroom. He was acquitted in 1985 of tax evasion and fraud, and in 1998 for insurance fraud against Lloyd's of London.

A triumphant King emerged from the latter outside the federal courthouse in New York with a wide smile on his face, never tired of beating the odds. "This is truly a victory for one of the greatest nations in the world," he said.

It was definitely another victory for Don King.

"I see my hair, a burning bush basted in righteous juices. . . . For now, my hair has mastered the universe! When I gaze into the mirror, I never cease to amaze myself. And I say this humbly."

CALIFORNIA, THERE HE GOES

Walter O'Malley

"The Dodgers aren't going to leave Brooklyn, are they Roy?" "Of course not. The Dodgers would never leave Brooklyn."

Going, going, gone. One might say that Walter O'Malley took the Dodgers deep. Just like hitting the long ball in baseball, O'Malley put one out of sight.

In this instance, an entire baseball team.

The last time Brooklyn baseball fans saw the Dodgers owner, he was headed out of town in a hurry with the franchise. *Their franchise.* It couldn't have been more disastrous if he had kidnapped a member of their own family. In fact, Brooklynites felt as if he had.

Left behind were millions of broken hearts. Up ahead were millions of new fans.

The year was 1958, and the destination was Los Angeles. Walter O'Malley had done the unthinkable: He had moved the popular Brooklyn Dodgers clear across the country to the West Coast. And if it wasn't enough to take away the beloved *Bums*, he convinced the rival New York Giants to make the move to California along with him.

This devious double play had Dodgers fans up in arms. "A lot of people wanted

to hang [O'Malley] in effigy," one newspaperman wrote. "Others wanted to hang him in person."

The Dodgers and Giants were the first major-league teams to play in California, opening up a new world. For the first time, the national pastime had truly gone national. Certainly other franchises had been moved before, but out of economic necessity. The Dodgers were a profitable and powerful franchise. From 1947–'57, they won six pennants and a World Series. For a good part of the 1940s and 1950s, baseball had been a New York-dominated game featuring three of the most powerful clubs: the Dodgers, Giants and New York Yankees. The major leagues were limited geographically. Most of the teams were in the northeast, and with the exception of St. Louis, none west of the Mississippi.

Then along came O'Malley to change the face of baseball…. and pro sports.

When the teenage Walter O'Malley suffered a broken nose playing baseball at a military academy, he might have thought it was his last contact with the sport. A native New Yorker, he graduated from law school the hard way, attending classes at night and working as an engineer during the day. He wore many hats: lawyer, engineer and director of the Brooklyn Borough Gas Company. His entry into baseball was pretty much through the backdoor. One of his clients, the Brooklyn Trust Company, held most of a $1.2 million debt by the financially troubled Dodgers. O'Malley, a bankruptcy expert, was asked to step in and help with the team's legal affairs during the Depression years of the early 1930s.

The Dodgers had only won two pennants since the World Series started in 1903. Larry MacPhail, who had revived the fortunes of the Cincinnati Reds, came to Brooklyn in the late '30s to do the same for the Dodgers. He refurbished inadequate Ebbets Field, installed lights and hired classy broadcaster Red Barber, with his Southern drawl, as the "Voice of the Dodgers." He also brought in good ballplayers. The Dodgers, who finished seventh in 1938, actually won the pennant in 1941.

The Dodgers' faithful fans, known as "the Flock," now had something to flock around, and they roared through the turnstiles. For four straight years, the Dodgers averaged over 1 million fans at one of the smallest ballparks in the majors.

O'Malley, a sharp businessman who had established his own engineering firm and made an astounding $50,000 in his first year in the wake of the Depression, envisioned greater things for the Dodgers—and himself.

When MacPhail stepped out, O' Malley stepped in. He purchased the team in 1944 along with club general manager and president Branch Rickey and John L. Smith, a Brooklyn chemical manufacturer. The trio wound up owning 75 percent of the Dodgers for about $1 million. Some fifty years later, on the other side of the continent, the O'Malley family would relinquish control of the Dodgers for $350 million.

Rickey, who had helped the St. Louis Cardinals rise to prominence in the 1930s with the best farm system in baseball, outdid himself with the Dodgers.

The Dodgers and Giants were the first major-league teams to play in California, opening up a new world. For the first time, the national pastime had truly gone national.

For four straight years, the Dodgers averaged over 1 million fans at one of the smallest ballparks in the majors.

Rickey broke baseball's color barrier when he brought in several fine black players, including the trailblazing Jackie Robinson.

Although O'Malley is never mentioned in regard to the Dodgers' "great experiment" involving black players, he had as much at stake financially as Rickey. "I'm sure they talked it over," said Tom Lasorda, the longtime manager of the Dodgers in Los Angeles. "There's no question that O'Malley should have shared in the credit. He was the guy who did everything for the black players in spring training that they wouldn't have gotten otherwise. He made them all feel like they were an important part of the organization."

Everyone but Robinson, it seemed. In his autobiography, *I Never Had It Made*, Robinson said O'Malley was antagonistic toward him. Robinson had reason to feel this way when the all-business O'Malley traded him to the Giants after the 1956 season. Rather than play for the Dodgers' hated arch-rivals, and nearing the end of his career, Robinson retired.

By that time, O'Malley had taken control of the Dodgers, buying out the shares of both his partners. Unhappy with the run-down conditions at Ebbets Field, O'Malley pushed for a new domed stadium at the vital intersection of Flatbush Avenue and Atlantic, in the very heart of Brooklyn. The city would have to condemn the land in order to give it to the Dodgers, and O'Malley's plan was rejected. When Brooklyn officials suggested the site of the 1939 World's Fair in Queens as an alternative, O'Malley started looking for an alternative city.

Los Angeles had earlier lured pro football to its environs. Getting the Dodgers for L.A. would be the topper. O'Malley was offered a deal he couldn't refuse, and by the end of the 1956 season, had agreed to move his club west. The Dodgers' last year in Brooklyn would be 1957. It was top-secret stuff as O'Malley worked behind the scenes.

O'Malley then pulled off his biggest coup—using his well-known persuasive talents to convince New York Giants owner Horace Stoneham that he absolutely had to move his team to the West Coast with him. With Stoneham's team in San Francisco, a natural California rivalry would be created. O'Malley must have made a convincing argument. Stoneham had originally planned to move his team to Minneapolis.

Despite O'Malley's efforts, keeping things quiet during the 1957 season wasn't easy, and speculation was rife about a possible Dodgers move. Fans were concerned. One day after a game at Ebbets Field, an anxious young fan approached Dodgers catcher Roy Campanella outside the park with the question that was on everyone's mind.

"The Dodgers aren't going to leave Brooklyn, are they, Roy?" he asked.

"Of course not," Campanella replied, "the Dodgers would never leave Brooklyn."

That's what everyone thought. It would never happen.

Until it did.

"Dodgers And Giants Move West," the headlines blared. One New York newspaper featured the cartoon drawing of the "Brooklyn Bum" going Hollywood, lying by a pool and soaking up the sun.

The team played its first game on April 18 at Memorial Coliseum, defeating the San Francisco Giants 6-5. Within the next year, they would defeat the Chicago White Sox to win a world championship.

Los Angeles gave O'Malley the keys to the city, and prime real estate to build Dodger Stadium. The setting was ideal for baseball—beautiful mountains in the distance, exotic palm trees swaying in the breeze and perfect weather. Dodger Stadium would soon be considered the crown jewel of major-league ballparks. The Dodgers became the first team to draw 3 million, and consolidated O'Malley's status as he became baseball's most powerful owner.

"His fellow owners relied on him in terms of direction and major policy decisions to an extent you wouldn't believe...." said Marvin Miller, at the time executive director of the Players Association.

O'Malley stretched the boundaries for others to follow, not just west and not only in baseball. The Cleveland Rams had moved to Los Angeles in the 1940s to set up an NFL presence on the West Coast, but hardly made a ripple on the national sports landscape. The Dodgers' dash along with the Giants' to the West Coast, meanwhile, was a watershed. It occurred in an era when baseball was at the height of its popularity. It involved two enormously popular New York teams. The Dodgers' success story encouraged expansion and the movement of franchises in all sports.

The Most Hated Man in Brooklyn had become the Pied Piper of the sports world.

The Dodgers became the first team to draw 3 million, and consolidated O'Malley's status as he became baseball's most powerful owner.

THE SPRINTER AND THE MILER

Jesse Owens and Roger Bannister

For them, no achievement was unreachable. It just had yet to be reached.

When Jesse Owens looked around the Olympic Stadium in Berlin, he saw obstacles. So he sprinted through them. When Roger Bannister began his races, the barrier was invisible, an artificial obstruction created by others in which Bannister never believed. So he ran right through it.

Owens, the greatest sprinter of his day—perhaps any day—and Bannister, the first man to conquer the 4-minute mile, proved that there was no such thing as an impossible goal. For them, no achievement was unreachable. It just had yet to be reached.

Owens was already a highly decorated athlete before the 1936 Olympics. A year before, in a one-day Big Ten meet at Michigan, Owens shook off back pain and tied the world record in the 100-yard dash. His tender back limited how many long jumps he could take, so he went all-out on his first leap—and sailed 26 feet, 8 1/4 inches, breaking the world mark by 6 inches (a record that held until 1960).

Moments later, with little rest after his incredible jump, Owens ran a 20.3 in the 220 dash, yet another world mark. And he finished off the most remarkable day in track history by running the 220-yard hurdles in 22.6 seconds. Yep, another world mark.

His appearance at the Berlin Games was steeped in controversy. In fact, the United States considered boycotting the games, but Avery Brundage, the despotic head of the U.S. Olympic Committee, opposed it. So the Americans went to Germany.

What they found was mass hysteria, a dictator who wanted to use the Games as proof of his "Aryan Master Race" theory, and a German team that indeed, did extremely well. But the Germans couldn't stop Jesse Owens. Nobody could, and it humiliated Chancellor Adolf Hitler, whose warped views included labeling blacks as "subhumans."

Owens' superhuman performance began with the 100-meter dash. Hitler predicted Erich Borchmeyer would win. Owens roared to a world record, 10.3 seconds. The German didn't medal.

On that first day of triumph for the American, Hitler didn't stick around to congratulate Owens, although "Der Führer" had done so for other athletes, mostly Germans. But there are conflicting views on whether Hitler snubbed the American, as the U.S. media claimed, or had been advised by International

... the Germans couldn't stop Jesse Owens. Nobody could, and it humiliated Chancellor Adolf Hitler

—by winning, Owens had effectively demolished Hitler's notion of Aryan supremacy.

Olympic Committee members that he had to offer the same kudos to every black winner, or to none.

Regardless, Owens wasn't done winning, and Hitler wasn't done fuming. The next day, in the long jump, Owens struggled to qualify—he was given one foul even though he was only warming up on the runway—and then found himself in a tight duel with Germany's Lutz Long. As Hitler watched through binoculars, Long tied Owens' best effort, 25 feet 9 1/2 inches. With the crowd roaring in delight, Owens took off his sweat suit, calmly strode to the runway and jumped beyond 26 feet.

Long could not match that effort, and Owens, already the winner, added a majestic leap of 26 feet 5 1/4 inches, an Olympic record, for his second gold. He and Long walked around the stadium arm in arm, celebrating their medals, as Hitler scowled.

Next for Owens, later in the day, was the 200 meters, where he set yet another world record, 20.7, the first sub-21-second performance. By now, Owens was being celebrated as the greatest runner in Olympic history, which he clearly was.

Celebrated everywhere but in Germany, where a Nazi official complained to the American government for using "subhuman Negro athletes" to win races.

Owens was not scheduled to run in the 400-meter relay, but American coach Lawson Robertson defied the criteria of the U.S. Olympic Trials in which the fourth through seventh place finishers would comprise the relay team. He dropped Marty Glickman and Sam Stoller, inserting Owens and Ralph Metcalfe.

Glickman and Stoller were Jewish, and Glickman claimed Brundage didn't want

to offend the Germans if the Americans won the race with two Jews. Glickman long asserted that Owens argued vehemently against the decision. But Robertson would not—or could not—reverse it, and Owens led off the relay that established one more world record, 39.8 seconds.

Jesse Owens owned four gold medals. He never did get to meet Hitler.

But the fact that Hitler chose to ignore the black American athlete's accomplishments, according to sports historian Kevin Grace, is exactly the point—by winning, Owens had effectively demolished Hitler's notion of Aryan supremacy.

"Jesse had the most impact of any sports hero of the decade," said Grace. "Everyone knew what Hitler stood for. And right there in front of Hitler… [Owens] reaffirmed traditional American values, giving Depression America something it could brag about to the rest of the world."

"Jesse gave hope to people during the Depression, especially black people," his wife, Ruth Owens, recalled after he died in 1980. "Places they had never been before, blacks were able to go because of him."

Not quite.

Owens himself could not parlay his magnificent achievements into anything substantial back home. Racism wasn't as widely broadcast as in Hitler's warped world, but it was definitely present in America. After a ticker-tape parade in New York, Owens couldn't get a steady job. The hero was not hirable because of the color of his skin? Absurd, but true.

"Jesse never received the financial rewards for what he accomplished," Ruth Owens said, noting that her husband's jobs ranged from page boy at the Ohio state building to play-ground instructor to carnival sideshow participant when he sprinted against racehorses.

But what he achieved could not be overshadowed. Eventually, Owens got his due, including the Medal of Freedom, presented by President Ford in 1976. In 1990, a posthumous Congressional Gold Medal was awarded to Owens' wife by President Bush.

Owens' legacy came full circle in 1996 during the buildup to the Atlanta Olympics. When the official torch run came through his hometown of Oakville, Alabama, a dedication was held for Jesse Owens Memorial Park, built in a field where Owens and his sharecropper family once picked cotton. For years, local blacks had tried to raise money for the park, but could collect only about $150,000. The torch run ignited interest in the project, and more than $1.3 million in donations flowed in.

The centerpiece is a bronze statue of Owens running though the Olympic rings, a fitting tribute to the man who soared beyond the hatred and racism of his day.

For Bannister, the idea of a 4-minute mile hardly was implausible. Sure, he knew the world record of 4:01.4 had stood for nine years. But Bannister, who once quit track to play rugby, was equipped with the perfect weapon to destroy the myth built around breaking 4:00: His mind.

"Gundar Haegg held the world record, and the fact that it stuck for nine years was used as an argument for some people to say, 'Well, there has to be a barrier somewhere. Maybe this is the barrier,'" Bannister said. "I had no doubt this idea of not running under four minutes was ridiculous, a mental block established to explain failure."

Certainly, Bannister needed the physical tools—speed, strength, stamina—to

Eventually, Owens got his due, including the Medal of Freedom, presented by President Ford in 1976. In 1990, a posthumous Congressional Gold Medal was awarded to Owens' wife by President Bush.

"I had no doubt this idea of not running under four minutes was ridiculous, a mental block established to explain failure."

challenge the supposedly unchallengeable. But his background in medicine (he would later become a doctor) led to experimentation in training methods that helped him run faster. In his first training mile at Oxford University in 1946, he was timed in 4:53. But in his first competition for the school, after several months of workouts, he was down to 4:30.8.

"I knew with the proper training, I could go much faster," he said. "As it became clear that somebody was going to … run under four minutes, I felt that I would prefer it to be me." No doubt.

But first came a bitter disappointment in the 1952 Olympics, where Bannister was fourth in a 1,500-meter race he believed he should have won. Failing to win an Olympic medal intensified his desire to break the 4-minute record.

As the track season opened in 1954, Bannister's training had gone so well that he was in peak shape. In a meet matching Oxford's athletes against representatives of the British Amateur Athletic Association, for whom Bannister competed, he would race against not only some formidable runners, but against the clock.

This time, he vowed, the clock would lose.

For years, athletes who broke through supposedly insurmountable barriers were said to have pulled a Roger Bannister.

The first lap was run in 57.5 seconds. A 60.7 lap followed, and they were at 3:00.4 heading into the final quarter-mile.

"At that point, it became a battle of the mind, not the body," Bannister said. "The world seemed to stand still and I had no energy left, yet I kept running quicker and quicker to the finish line."

He leaped at the tape, breaking it and collapsing into teammates' arms. Bannister knew he could not run any faster. If this wasn't under four minutes, well, maybe there was something to this barrier stuff.

Moments later, the track announcer said: "The result of the one mile, won by Roger Bannister in a time of 3 ..."

No one could hear the rest of the announcement. Bannister's time was 3:59.4, but that one mere digit, that 3 at the outset of the official clocking was all anyone needed to hear.

"It was a wonderful, memorable moment," he said. "It also was a record that would not last."

Indeed, just seven weeks later, Bannister's closest rival in the race to break the 4-minute mile, John Landy, would break it.

Still, it was Bannister's comfort with the challenge and confidence in his ability to handle it that made his achievement monumental. For years, athletes who broke through supposedly insurmountable barriers were said to have pulled a Roger Bannister.

So who will the next Bannister be? It won't be someone getting under 3 minutes in the mile.

"The human race," he said, "without genetic experimentation, will not break 3 minutes."

THE TENNIS ACE
Arthur Ashe

He was one of those rare athletes whose achievements away from the arena far outweighed what he accomplished in his chosen profession.

It wasn't as if Arthur Ashe was the best tennis player of his time. There was always a Rod Laver, John Newcombe or Jimmy Connors in the way. But Ashe—whose journey went from the segregated tennis courts of Richmond to a championship on the storied grass at Wimbledon—was nevertheless the most significant tennis player of his era, perhaps any era. He spoke out for himself, his peers, athletes in general and, of course, his race.

In everything Ashe did, he made a difference. No cause was too insignificant, no challenge too daunting. He was one of those rare athletes whose achievements away from the arena far outweighed what he accomplished in his chosen profession. And what he accomplished was impressive and courageous.

He won the very first U.S. Open in 1968. That tournament allowed professionals and amateurs to compete for the first time, and the pros were heavy favorites. Ashe stormed through the tournament, upsetting the likes of Roy Emerson and Cliff Drysdale before outlasting Tom Okker in a brutal five-set final. But more significantly, Ashe became the first black man to win a Grand Slam title.

"I hope in the near future, the color of my skin or anyone's skin isn't even something that is mentioned," Ashe said. By the time Ashe died on February 6, 1993, of AIDS contracted from a blood transfusion, his hope had been realized.

"Arthur was a true American hero," President Clinton said of him, "and a great example to us all."

Born in a blacks-only hospital in Richmond, Virginia, on July 10, 1943, Arthur was the son of a security guard for the parks department. While Arthur Jr. began playing tennis on his own, Arthur Sr. taught his son an important lesson that would never be forgotten.

"Drummed into me above all, by my dad, by the whole family, was that without your good name, you would be nothing," Ashe said. But he would have to make his name outside of Richmond, where segregation laws severely limited opportunities. He traveled to Lynchburg to play on the private court of Dr. Robert Walter Johnson, who had coached Althea Gibson. Johnson became Ashe's conduit to black tennis tournaments throughout the region.

"One of the basic lessons from Dr. Johnson was to behave

well, no matter how things were going in a match," Ashe said. He learned that lesson well, too, and, for his entire career, Ashe was considered the sport's most gentlemanly player.

Ashe traveled outside of Richmond regularly in order to compete against whites, and in 1957 was the first African American to play in the Maryland boys' championships. It was also Ashe's first integrated event. In his senior year, tired of Richmond's segregated tennis, he moved to St. Louis and enrolled in high school there.

By the time he was recruited by UCLA, Ashe was one of the top junior players in the nation. In college, he refined his game, and by 1963, he was good enough to be selected to the American Davis Cup squad—the first African-American man so honored. In '65, he led the Bruins to the national championship.

... by 1963, he was good enough to be selected to the American Davis Cup squad—the first African-American man so honored.

For the next decade, Ashe would be a mainstay of U.S. tennis. Two weeks before winning the 1968 U.S. Open, he became the first black to take the U.S. men's singles championships. He finished that year as the highest-ranked American.

In 1969, Ashe applied for a visa to play in the South African Open, and was denied. His call for South Africa's expulsion from the International Lawn Tennis Federation and Davis Cup play because of the nation's policy of apartheid, was supported by many prominent individuals and organizations, in and out of the tennis arena. Three years would pass before Ashe would be granted his visa, after which he became the first black pro to play in South Africa's national championships. (Fifteen years later, still fighting the good fight as co-chairman of the group Artists and Athletes Against Apartheid that promoted a boycott of South Africa by performers and sports figures, he and 46 others were arrested in anti-apartheid protests at the South African Embassy in Washington.)

There were many more firsts—and victories—on the court: the 1970 Australian Open crown; the 1971 French Open doubles title with Marty Riessen; and the greatest victory of all, a stunning upset of Connors at Wimbledon in 1975: 6-1, 6-1, 5-7, 6-4. Ashe won 33 tournaments from 1968-'78 and went 28-6 in the Davis Cup, playing on four U.S. championship teams.

Ashe married Jeanne Moutoussamy in 1977; two years later, he suffered a heart attack at a tennis clinic in New York and underwent quadruple bypass surgery. He retired from competitive tennis in 1980, four months later. As captain of the U.S. team, he collected two more Davis Cup crowns, in 1981 and 1982. In 1985, he was inducted into the International Tennis Hall of Fame.

But there were dozens of other Halls of Fame where Ashe belonged.

Perhaps some literary Hall will induct him for his three-volume examination of the African-American sports scene, *A Hard Road To Glory*. Or for his memoir, *Days of Grace*. Certainly there is a place for Ashe, winner of the Omega Award in 1983 for determination of spirit and ability to overcome significant obstacles, in all kinds of humanitarian halls.

In 1986, at the grand old age of 34, Ashe became a father. Only two years later, his life would change once more, but this time, irrevocably.

After experiencing some numbness in his right hand, Ashe was hospitalized, and tests revealed toxoplasmosis, a bacterial infection often present in HIV-positive individuals. It was then that Ashe was diagnosed with HIV, the source of his exposure believed to be the blood transfusion he received during surgery in 1983. It was not until 1992 that Ashe called a press conference and went public with his condition.

During what turned out to be the last year of his life, Ashe was lauded for his speech at the United Nations in which he urged the world to embrace AIDS

Certainly there is a place for Ashe, winner of the Omega Award in 1983 for determination of spirit and ability to overcome significant obstacles …

awareness and rally in the battle against the disease that would claim his life so prematurely at age 49.

"Arthur believed in doing things right and in doing the right thing," said Donald Dell, his longtime friend and agent. "I can remember in his early days that he was not considered active enough, involved enough, militant enough. But Arthur certainly proved the opposite to be true."

More than 5,000 mourners filed past Ashe's casket as his body lay in state at the Governor's Mansion in Richmond, the first to do so since Confederate general Stonewall Jackson in 1863, and nearly 6,000 people attended his

*"He took the burden of the race and wore it as a cloak of dignity."
—Andrew Young*

funeral. Atlanta mayor and former U.N. ambassador Andrew Young delivered the eulogy, saying of Ashe: "He took the burden of the race and wore it as a cloak of dignity."

A bronze statue of Ashe now stands on Richmond's Monument Avenue, dedicated on the occasion of what would have been his 53rd birthday, joining the Confederate war heroes whose monuments line the street. Ashe is depicted holding a tennis racket above his head in his left hand and a book over his head in his right, with four bronze children gazing up at him.

Ashe and Richmond community projects leader Rayford L. Harris, sponsored Virginia Heroes Inc., in 1991. National and local role models met with sixth-grade students to talk about planning for the future. Harris remembered that Ashe was often the center of attention.

"For somebody like Arthur Ashe to come in and make the type of comments he did, that had to have a big impact on the kids," Harris said.

"And he didn't have to sound a trumpet. All those kids had to do was consider where it was coming from, and that was enough to get the message across."

For kids, for adults, for anyone, Arthur Ashe delivered the right message.

CLARKSVILLE COMET
Wilma Rudolph

Wilma Rudolph was waiting to make history. She stood on the track poised and ready to grab the baton. The scene was the 1960 Rome Olympics and she was about to complete the anchor leg of the 400-meter relay race. The twenty-year-old had already won the 100- and 200-meter races.

Her Tigerbelle teammates from Tennessee State were depending on her. "Hey, girl, you've already gotten your two medals," they kidded her before the relay. "You better get us this gold medal."

But as Rudolph's teammate, Lucinda Williams-Adams, approached with the baton, the handoff was far from a smooth one. "I knew she wasn't taking off, so I yelled for her to go," Williams-Adams recalled.

Rudolph was on her way, arms pumping furiously. The graceful, long-legged American runner started behind Germany's anchor leg, but soon caught up, an antelope overtaking her prey. She blazed ahead and completed a relay run of 44.5 seconds—almost as quick as the world-record 44.4 seconds she and her teammates from Tennessee State had set in the semifinals. Olympic gold belonged to the Americans.

When Rudolph crossed the finish line, she placed herself in a special category: the first American woman to win three gold medals at one Olympic Games. She also became an inspiration and example for other great African-American female athletes to follow, particularly in track and field.

And though she had never craved the spotlight, Rudolph also suddenly became the center of a lot of attention. Television was starting to make its presence felt in sports, and millions had seen Rudolph's spectacular Olympic performance. When Rudolph and her teammates competed in Europe after the Olympics, fans flocked to see this popular new star, christened "The Black Pearl" by newspapers. In Cologne, Germany, the Rudolph hysteria hit new heights. There were stories that fans beat their fists on her bus until she acknowledged them with a wave. There was a story that a fan even stole her shoes off her feet.

Her homecoming, shared with another Olympic hero, boxer Cassius Clay, was memorable. On a visit to Lexington, Kentucky, Rudolph and Clay rode around town in a pink Cadillac convertible as thousands cheered. "[Clay] kept holler-

> *When Rudolph crossed the finish line, she placed herself in a special category: the first American woman to win three gold medals at one Olympic Games.*

ing, 'Wilma Rudolph! Here's Wilma Rudolph!'" Rudolph recalled. "I kept sliding down in the seat."

There would be no hiding for Rudolph from that point on. She had set the standard for other American female track stars, quite simply as "the world's fastest woman."

Rudolph's family had always believed in her, and had prayed for her to succeed. But their prayers had not been for her athletic achievements. They were praying she would survive.

The 20th of 22 children, Rudolph was born prematurely at four and a half pounds in St. Bethlehem, Tennessee, on June 23, 1940. Her disadvantaged childhood in Clarksville, Tennessee, was a series of never-ending medical problems. At four years old, she was stricken with double pneumonia, followed by scarlet fever. "We thought she would die," said her mother, Blanche Rudolph. Polio followed, and doctors predicted she would never walk again. They were wrong.

Wilma's determined mother took her twice a week by bus to Meharry, the black medical college at Fisk University in Nashville—fifty miles away, but the closest hospital for blacks. The doctors there taught Mrs. Rudolph physical therapy exercises for the family to do at home. Family members massaged Wilma's legs several times a day to make them stronger. "All I can remember is being ill and bedridden," Rudolph once said. "I wore braces and couldn't walk until I was nine." And even then, she had the help of an orthopedic shoe. Not until the age of 11, was Rudolph finally able to walk unaided.

At which point she started making up for all that lost time.

In junior high, Wilma joined the basketball team, though it was three years before the coach put her in a game, as a starting guard. When the coach resurrected the track team, Rudolph ran in the 50 meters, 75 meters, 100 meters, and

At four years old, she was stricken with double pneumonia, followed by scarlet fever . . . Polio followed, and doctors predicted she would never walk again.

Skinny and angular, she picked up the nickname "Skeeter," short for mosquito.

the relay events, excelling at them all. In fact, Wilma's desire to express herself on a track often caused a conflict with her schooling.

"So many days, I pretended I was sick in class," she said. "The teachers would let me out and I'd go jump over the fence into the stadium. … and start running."

At Burt High School in Clarksville, while a sophomore, Rudolph broke the state basketball record for girls. By then, she had sprouted to nearly six feet and become a star basketball player. Skinny and angular, she picked up the nickname "Skeeter," short for mosquito. Her speed and leaping ability caught the attention of Tennessee State track coach Ed Temple, and a track star was born.

At the age of 15, Rudolph was already grabbing attention when she dominated the 1955 National AAU Championships. At 16, she won an Olympic medal when her relay team finished third for a bronze at the 1956 Games in Melbourne. She was disappointed that she did not win a gold medal in Melbourne, admitting, "My whole world was crushed until we got the bronze medal in the relay."

Four years later, it appeared her world was going to be crushed again. The day before her first race at the 1960 Rome Olympics, she sprained her ankle while practicing. She cried from the pain. " … I thought I had broken it, and that everything was down the drain now."

It must have reawakened her childhood determination not to let anything stop

The inner strength that had enabled a little girl to learn to walk despite the odds, to win battles over poverty, illness, racism and sexism —all of it served as an example even after Rudolph's death.

her. Running with her ankle taped, she breezed to victory in the 100- and 200-meter races, leaving her competition trailing far behind. Then she combined with Tigerbelle teammates Martha Hudson, Barbara Jones and Williams-Adams to win the relay race. Afterward, the "World's Fastest Woman" made history in another way, by insisting that her homecoming parade in Clarksville be an integrated event—the first in that city's history. She also broke ground in other areas, becoming the first woman to be invited to many of the nation's top track and field events that previously had been a male-only domain.

Rudolph felt there was no way she could top her performance in the Olympics, and declined a repeat appearance in the 1964 Games. Now retired from competitive track, she went into teaching and charity work, helping children to overcome obstacles. She married her high school sweetheart and had four children of her own. She was a welcome guest speaker at dozens of schools and universities, and also did sports commentary on TV.

A community activist since the sixties, she worked with Vice President Hubert Humphrey on Operation Champion, a program designed to take star athletes from 16 of the largest city ghettoes in the country and give them professional training. Rudolph became one of the track specialists. She also founded the Wilma Rudolph Foundation to support underprivileged youth, and to provide free coaching and academic assistance.

In 1994, she succumbed to brain cancer at age 54. Her dedication to her sport inspired other great female athletes, such as Jackie Joyner-Kersee and Florence Griffith Joyner. The inner strength that had enabled a little girl to learn to walk despite the odds, to win battles over poverty, illness, racism and sexism—all of it served as an example even after Rudolph's death.

"Whenever I was down … I often thought how dedicated Wilma was to overcome the obstacles," Griffith Joyner said. "That motivated me to push harder."

THE MOUTH THAT ROARED
Howard Cosell

There was the bluster. Always, the bluster. There were the self-important pronouncements, the self-congratulations, and the self-assuredness that he, above everyone else, was correct—regardless of the subject.

And there was the ever-present verbal needle, which he dug into friend and foe. Whether playfully jabbing at Muhammad Ali, poking fun at "Dandy Don" Meredith, his comical sidekick on "Monday Night Football", or sticking an oral dagger into print journalists, the mouth was his best weapon.

Howard Cosell used words the way armies use artillery. He let fly with barrage after barrage, trying to get his scatter shots to hit a target. Any target.

Often, he was right on line. Almost as often, he was lost in the wilderness. But he was entertaining, and controversial, and without him, television sports might still be nothing more than fun and games.

"Howard Cosell was one of the most original people ever to appear on American television," Roone Arledge said. "He became a giant by the simple act of telling the truth in an industry that was not used to hearing it and considered it revolutionary."

And he did it with a personality that irritated some, enraged others.

"Arrogant, pompous, obnoxious, vain, cruel, verbose, a show-off . . . of course I am."

"Arrogant, pompous, obnoxious, vain, cruel, verbose, a show-off. I have been called all of these. Of course I am," Cosell said. "Telling it like it is, that's all I've ever done in my career, whether it was Muhammad Ali's stand against the abuse of his civil rights, or the very farce that boxing became, or the shamateurism of the Olympics. I've taken on all comers, and I've prospered."

All of Cosell's foibles should not obscure just how much television sports prospered with him in the lead. For years, he was the lightning rod in a journalistic battle in which—Cosell claimed—he had no allies.

While most of the electronic media accepted the words of team management, athletes, coaches and officials as gospel, Cosell sometimes saw it as heresy. For decades, "homerism" was accepted in broadcast sports. Cosell shattered it by criticizing everyone he deemed deserving of criticism. That meant just about everyone, and much of the time, he was right.

"Every person working in sports journalism today owes a tremendous debt to Howard Cosell," Arledge added. "His greatest contribution was elevating sports reporting out of daily play-by-play and placing it in the larger context of society."

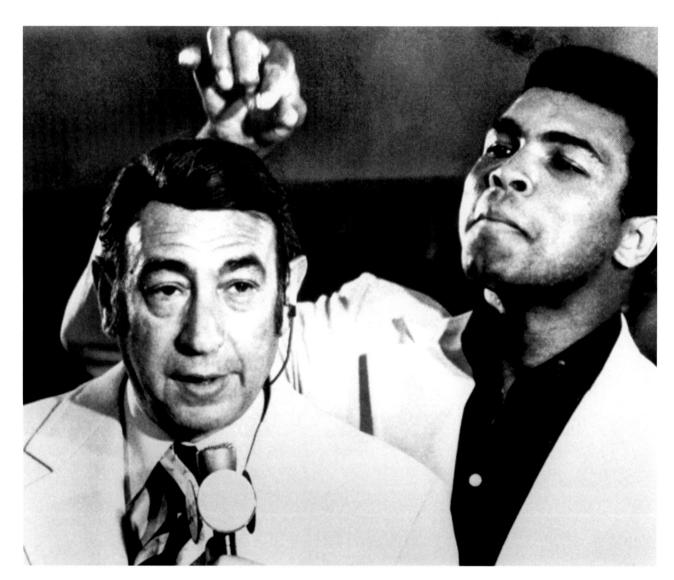

Even the people he covered, those he lambasted on the air in his national forums on ABC-TV and radio—or on "Monday Night Football", where he gained his most fame and helped that program become the most successful in TV sports history—found something they liked about Cosell. Amidst all the presumptuousness and pomposity, he was forthright.

Whatever Cosell said, he meant it. Every polysyllabic word of it.

"He was loud, boisterous and extreme, but he really got people's attention and he was really bright," Billie Jean King said.

"He made people listen. He certainly made people think and he made people watch," added television executive Dennis Lewin. "You didn't always agree with Howard, but he was never afraid to say what he thought.

"Howard broke the mold when it came to sportscasters. He was very intelligent, plus he was a master showman and a master entertainer."

Not that Cosell would want anyone to remember the ill-fated variety show he hosted. Or his clownish performance, as himself, in the Woody Allen film *Bananas*.

Whatever Cosell said, he meant it. Every polysyllabic word of it.

"His greatest contribution was elevating sports reporting out of daily play-by-play and placing it in the larger context of society."

No, Cosell, who died in 1995, would want to be remembered for grilling interviewees over a slow flame. For leading the charge to have pro boxing outlawed. For turning a law degree, an aggressive nature and a pedantic personality into a ground-breaking career.

Born Howard William Cohen on March 25, 1918, in Winston-Salem, N.C., Cosell was the son of a Polish immigrant and the grandson of a rabbi. The family later moved to Brooklyn.

In 1972, when he was covering the Munich Olympics, he was returning to his apartment near the stadium when he was told that Israeli athletes were being held hostage.

"All of a sudden I realized there was a concentration camp right outside of Munich during the war and, my god, it is happening again," he said. "I remembered I was a Jewish boy from Brooklyn and decided to do something about it."

What he did was provide superb coverage of the tragedy, even talking his way into the athletes' village by pretending to be a salesman for Puma, the company that supplied the athletes with equipment and shoes.

Cosell actually wanted to be a newspaper reporter before turning to law, which he practiced for a decade. But in 1953, he became a stringer for ABC Radio and, in 1956, turned to broadcasting full-time, mainly because of his "romantic ideas" about sports and his flair for communications. He began locally in New York, but soon built a reputation for not pulling punches, and the networks came calling.

Cosell delivered his pointed commentaries with a nasal voice that often grated on his listeners. But it also fascinated them, even if, many times, the words he used and the phrases he concocted were difficult to understand. Everyone who ever heard Cosell exclaim, "This is a tra-ves-ty of mon-u-ment-al pro-por-tions," would be back for more sooner or later.

For several years running, Cosell was voted the most popular sportscaster in America. And, at the same time, the least popular.

For several years running, Cosell was voted the most popular sportscaster in America. And, at the same time, the least popular.

Millions of fans tuned into "Monday Night Football" not just to see the Packers and Cowboys and Steelers, but to hear Cosell's harangues of various NFL types. Viewers eagerly awaited the jocular barbs Cosell exchanged with Meredith, who might have been the only former athlete-turned-broadcaster that Cosell respected.

He became close with Ali, Pete Rozelle and, yes, even with several sports writers, despite his disgust with the profession in general. But during the last ten years of his life—perhaps due to the cancellation of his award-winning investigative show, "Sportsbeat," in 1985—Cosell inexplicably cut himself off. In his retirement, he distanced himself from his former colleagues and their sports—notably pro football and boxing—railing against the "poisoned professions" they had become in his eyes.

Might Cosell, who was a bitter man when he died at age 77, have had as big an impact as a lawyer as he did in television? Perhaps, but not likely.

Two days after his death, Cosell received an Emmy Award for his "perceptive and courageous observation of the sports world" and his "unfailing high standards of excellence."

"He has given the public and his peers a heritage that will endure for generations to come," the citation said.

And it has.

THE VISIONARY
Roone Arledge

Roone Arledge didn't create the world of drama in sports. He simply perfected the manner by which the thrill of victory and the agony of defeat have been presented.

In 1972, less than 24 hours after 11 Israeli athletes were murdered in Munich in one of the ugliest tragedies in sports—and Olympic Games history—Roone Arledge defied his employers at ABC and had his staff compile a 40-minute documentary on the massacre.

The network told him to scrap it.

Instead, he broadcast the entire documentary at the end of the day's Olympic programming schedule. Uninterrupted. In direct opposition to his bosses at ABC and against the wishes of the International Olympic Committee.

"There was no other choice," he said. "The story needed to be told, then and there."

It was the way the stories were told that made ABC unique. And it was the way Arledge viewed television's role in sports coverage that altered forever the relationship of media and athlete.

Roone Arledge didn't create the world of drama in sports. He simply perfected the manner by which the thrill of victory and the agony of defeat have been presented. From Olympic scandals and tragedies, to miracles on ice, on grass and on court, the ground-breaking television sports executive rarely has taken a step back. Or even looked back.

Arledge brought us "Wide World of Sports." And "Monday Night Football." And Jim McKay. And Howard Cosell. He believed in how compelling sport can be, and had the courage to find new, challenging ways to televise it.

"Roone Arledge understands [that] television journalism has the tools with which to make significant statements about the world of sports," Cosell said. "To his everlasting credit, he lets people such as myself make those statements, present the facts, tell it like it is."

Arledge hardly appeared headed for such a noteworthy position when he began his TV career with the Dumont network as a production assistant. Dumont folded in 1955, and he went to NBC as a stage manager. Arledge produced a Saturday morning kids show, "Hi Mom," with Shari Lewis, which would win an Emmy.

By 1957, he was producing sports at ABC, which was a weak third among the networks. So Arledge had to be aggressive and innovative.

He found his early niche by gobbling up events outside the

sporting mainstream. Track and field was especially enticing, but anything with a Cold War angle worked for him back then.

"In those days, if you had an American against a Russian, it didn't matter what they were doing, they could have been kayaking, and people would watch," he said.

How many sports owe their penetration into the sporting consciousness to Arledge? Through "Wide World of Sports," he enhanced golf's popularity by buying rights to the British Open. He introduced figure skating and gymnastics, thereby bringing the grace, beauty, power and precision of women athletes to the forefront.

Imagine if Arledge had ignored the sports that brought the world Peggy Fleming and Dorothy Hamill, Olga Korbut, Nadia Comaneci and Mary Lou Retton.

ABC's Olympic coverage would become its calling card. It chronicled the action in a dramatic way and gave it a heartbeat that humanized not only the athletes, but their events. A pole vault duel that carried deep into the night; a bevy of officiating blunders that cost the U.S. team a basketball gold medal; an outrageous leap into the Mexico City air that seemed to soar beyond the moon. ABC truly spanned the globe, and what it televised usually was unforgettable.

But the Olympics came only every four years, hardly enough sustenance to guarantee the survival of a network's sports department.

In 1960, ABC also began televising pro football with the AFL. It was during those games that on-screen graphics were used for the first time, and they became a staple in sports coverage. But by 1964, when it first became the TV home of the Olympics, ABC had been outbid for the AFL rights by NBC.

Arledge knew it was imperative to get pro football back on the network. The NFL had experimented with five Monday night telecasts on CBS, and commissioner Pete Rozelle was championing the idea of a regular Monday night series.

"There was something more dramatic about the games at night," Rozelle said. "It created an aura around the players and football itself."

More importantly, a regular prime-time forum allowed the NFL to attract an entirely new audience: women. And it catered to the casual fan, who was more interested in seeing the big names and top teams than the local clubs.

But ABC was third in the running: Although Arledge shared the same visions for pro football as did Rozelle, the commissioner felt an obligation to approach his current TV partners, CBS and NBC, while negotiating the new television deal in 1970 to coincide with the completion of the NFL-AFL merger.

"Pete went to CBS first," said NFL vice president Joe Browne. "CBS had a successful lineup then. Doris Day was on Monday nights at 9:30 and was wildly successful, and when he went to CBS, its president, Bob Wood said, 'And what, bump Doris Day?'

"Then he went to NBC, who was our new partner through the AFL, and they still had the successful Monday night movies.

"ABC was struggling and Roone had the vision to give it a shot."

Arledge couldn't be sure how hot a property he'd just acquired, but he knew

"Pete [Rozelle] went to CBS first … Doris Day was on Monday nights at 9:30 and was wildly successful, and when he went to CBS, its president, Bob Wood said, 'And what, bump Doris Day?'"

"We were desecrating the sacred game. CBS had Ray Scott, who was warm, friendly and informative. We had loudmouth Howard criticizing the coaches and management and the players and the play-calling. And we had Don kicking back and acting like he was at a family barbecue."

how to make it hotter. First, he insisted the league not have approval of his announcers, a policy that was in effect for the other networks. Rozelle said OK, and Arledge hired Cosell.

He teamed the acerbic Cosell with the down-home Texas charm of "Dandy" Don Meredith, a former NFL quarterback with a quick wit and absolutely no inhibitions. While Cosell raged, Meredith hummed country tunes.

"It was blasphemy," Arledge said with a laugh. "We were desecrating the sacred game. CBS had Ray Scott, who was warm, friendly and informative. We had loudmouth Howard criticizing the coaches and management and the players and the play-calling. And we had Don kicking back and acting like he was at a family barbecue."

The combination was perfect. It didn't hurt that the NFL was bypassing baseball as the No. 1 spectator sport in America, either.

"There was early criticism," Browne said. "Howard's career always was one where he was the favorite and the least favorite announcer in the polls—at the same time.

But he was the lightning rod, and that was good. It got the eyeballs to the TV, and the league was very supportive. Pete and Roone knew what Cosell could do."

Arledge knew what to do visually, too. "Monday Night Football" was treated as entertainment, with more cameras and graphics, a more festive atmosphere. It was a spectacle, not just a TV show.

Until Arledge, the prevailing opinion was that watching sports on TV was only a last-resort substitute for going to the ballpark. Therefore, the unspoken rule was to never present the game in a more attractive way than what fans could experience at the stadium. But Arledge gave home viewers the whole enchilada—and then some.

He pioneered the use of slow-motion replays after viewing a Japanese film that used the technique—albeit to glorify the gore of martial arts movies. He went stats crazy, providing the viewer with enough information to fill a week's worth of broadcasts, let alone three hours of prime-time football. With twelve cameras and tape machines on hand, the audience could see the plays from different angles, get instant replays, and see the reactions of players, coaches and fans.

"Monday Night Football" was on its way to becoming an institution. Arledge's idea—that sports could be presented as entertainment, like a concert or an opera—worked. That the party line could be replaced by investigative reporting and controversy. That the biggest sporting events—the Super Bowl, World Series, NCAA basketball championship, Olympics—drew big ratings and big bucks in prime time. In short, it changed the face of sports on television.

It changed pro football, too.

"The owners saw what television could do for them, and they saw the money they could get for playing at night," Arledge said. "They've never looked back."

Oh, Arledge wasn't infallible. For instance, he couldn't get the IOC and organizers of the 1980 Lake Placid Olympics to move the starting time of the U.S.-Soviet Union hockey game back into prime time. So instead of televising live the biggest victory in U.S.-Soviet sports history, ABC showed it on tape in prime time. But everybody has forgotten that in favor of the last ten seconds of the game and Al Michaels' memorable "Do you believe in miracles? Yes!!!!"

Arledge selected Keith Jackson, a college football man through and through, as the original play-by-play announcer on "Monday Night Football." And Arledge brought in the likes of Fred Williamson, Joe Namath and O.J. Simpson once Meredith got tired of the job.

More times, he has been right-on with his decisions, both as president of ABC Sports and, later, of ABC News. His concepts for covering sports are now the norm.

Without his influence, would we have round-the-clock sports programming all over the television dial? Sure, cable TV would have blossomed, but would sports have led the way?

"There have been comparable times in history when sports have been at the center of a culture and seemed to dominate the landscape," Arledge said. "Whether in Greek society or in what used to be called 'The Golden Age of Sport.' But everything is magnified by television."

And nobody could magnify it better.

Until Arledge, the prevailing opinion was that watching sports on TV was only a last-resort substitute for going to the ballpark.

THE GALLOPING GHOST, THE SLINGER AND THE PROFESSOR
Red Grange, Sammy Baugh, and Sid Luckman

"Almost single-handedly, Grange changed the perception of pro football from a circus into a serious enterprise."

Football, the prevailing opinion once said—no, shouted—would never be as popular as baseball in the United States. It would always lag behind the national pastime, played by every kid on diamonds across the nation from the time they can pick up a bat or toss a ball.

That opinion was at its strongest in the glory days of the Babe and the Murderers Row of the 1920s, or in the era of Joe D. and Ted Williams in the 1940s.

"He was the idol of all Illinois sports fans, from the day he ran wild against Michigan, and throughout his career."

It seems like folly today, when youngsters are as easily attracted to the gridiron, the soccer field, basketball court or ice rink as to the baseball field. It is especially ludicrous from a spectators' viewpoint, where football—yes, the game that couldn't possibly present a challenge—is the heralded king.

Credit goes to three men who long ago established football's popularity and built the foundation on which the NFL and the college game has established itself: Red Grange, Sammy Baugh, and Sid Luckman.

Grange was the sport's first big star, and he made his name in the time of Babe Ruth, Jack Dempsey and Bill Tilden—some heavyweight competition. Before Harold "Red" Grange attended the University of Illinois, college football was akin to the high school variety: localized and sparsely attended. By the time Grange left the Illini to join the fledgling NFL in 1925, he had been dubbed "The Galloping Ghost" by renowned sports writer Grantland Rice, and his No. 77 had become the most famous in sports.

Already nicknamed the "Wheaton Iceman" because he delivered ice in his Illinois hometown, Grange was a three-sport star (football, track, baseball) who stuck to football at Illinois. His first varsity game was remarkable, a three-touch-down performance built on speed and moves rarely seen.

In 1924, long before any wire service polls or national championship show-downs existed, Illinois and Michigan were considered the top teams in the nation. Both were undefeated the previous year. On October 18, at Illinois, a crowd of more than 67,000 expected Michigan coach Fielding Yost to devise a worthy defense to deal with Grange. Instead, Grange galloped for touchdowns of 95 yards on the opening kickoff, then 67, 56, 45, and 12 yards. Four of his scores came in the first 12 minutes. He also threw for a TD, accounted for 402 yards and pretty much single-handedly destroyed the Wolverines.

Even Yost was moved by that performance.

"If anyone ever has had a greater game of football, I have never heard of it," he said.

"He was the idol of all Illinois sports fans, from the day he ran wild against Michigan, and throughout his career," said Charles E. Flynn, a former Illinois sports information director. "He did a great deal for the university . . . through the inspiration he gave young people."

There was, however, another world to conquer. Although Illinois coach Bob Zuppke adamantly argued against Grange turning pro, a $100,000 offer from the Chicago Bears made Grange's choice easy.

His task as a pro was not. He had no other stars to aid him as he attempted to boost the popularity of the professional game, which routinely drew crowds ten times smaller than the throngs that flocked to college football stadiums.

Grange was more than up to the challenge.

With Grange in the Bears' lineup, 36,000 turned up at Wrigley Field for a Thanksgiving Day game with the Cardinals. When Bears owner George Halas scheduled a barnstorming tour across the football landscape—at one point, the team played seven games in nine days—the stands were packed.

"I'd play 25 or 30 games a year. Not all league games, but we traveled all over,"

Grange said. "You name it and we played football there. I probably played in every state in the 1920s."

At the Polo Grounds in New York, his run beat the host Giants, yet the fans—estimated at more than 65,000, including some who crashed through the gates when all the tickets had been sold—cheered for the Bears star.

"You're talking about bellwether players who can make an enormous difference in a given game, and even more important, how a game comes to be perceived," said Robert Baade, an economics professor at Lake Forest (Ill.) College who studied the financial impact of sports. "Almost single-handedly, Grange changed the perception of pro football from a circus into a serious enterprise."

So serious that Grange became a sporting icon. He was greeted by mayors and society bigwigs in every city. He attended social functions and hospital benefits that drew large crowds.

In 1926, noting how much money Halas was making off the tours, Grange and C.C. Pyle, his personal manager, asked for a share of the Bears. Halas refused, and Grange then sought an NFL franchise in New York. Unable to obtain that, he and Pyle began a competing league, the nine-team AFL, which lasted only one year. Grange played for the "Red Grange Yankees," who moved into the NFL as the New York Yankees when the AFL folded.

But Grange injured his knee in 1927 and also couldn't play in 1928. The Yankees disappeared, and Grange returned to the Bears in 1929. For the next six years, Grange was a mainstay of the "Monsters of the Midway" and still pro football's biggest attraction. No longer ghostlike in his moves, he remained a formidable player on offense and defense.

By then, the NFL was beyond taking baby steps. While still not on the level of baseball or even college football, it was headed in the right direction.

"In terms of impact, the only really comparable situation was Babe Ruth and what he did for baseball," Baade said of Grange's impact. "In that sense, you could say that Red Grange really was a legend in his own time."

Just as Grange's star was fading, Baugh's was rising out of the Texas plains. At Texas Christian University from 1934-'36, he earned the label "Slingin' Sammy" as he led the Horned Frogs to 29 victories, including Cotton Bowl and Sugar Bowl wins, and made All-America twice as he led the nation in passing.

Baugh was the game's first aerial genius. Dutch Meyer, his coach at TCU, had a way with words, once ordering his teams to "Fight 'em until hell freezes over, and then fight 'em on the ice."

He also said, "Sammy Baugh can throw a spiral through a West Texas tornado."

But Baugh was so much more than just a forerunner of John Unitas and Dan Marino. He was the best defensive back in college football, and one of its most reliable kickers. He was a superb leader.

"Back then, we had to play both ways. We had to do a lot of things, and you couldn't substitute in and out. You didn't have someone who just punted or kicked field goals," Baugh said.

He led the NFL in passing six times, and in 1943, provided Sunday afternoon relief from the headlines of war with perhaps the most remarkable season in league history —by leading the NFL in passing, punting and interceptions.

"Sammy Baugh
can throw a spiral
through a west
Texas tornado."

The NFL needed a big-time player to continue its development. Baugh was perfect. He led the Washington team to the championship in 1937, his first pro season. He spent 16 years with the Redskins, guiding them to five Eastern titles and two league championships. He led the NFL in passing six times, and in 1943, provided Sunday afternoon relief from the headlines of war with perhaps the most remarkable season in league history—by leading the NFL in passing, punting, and interceptions. In one game, against the Detroit Lions, Baugh passed for four touchdowns and intercepted four passes in a 42-20 victory.

Thanks to Slingin' Sammy, even after his retirement, pro football's star just kept rising.

Luckman was Baugh's contemporary, quarterbacking the Chicago Bears from 1939-1950. Unlike Baugh, the ultimate athlete, his role was more cerebral. If Halas—helped by Stanford coach Clark Shaughnessy—was the father of the modern offense, then Sid Luckman was the professor.

If not for Luckman's mastery of the T-formation, such Hall of Fame passers as Unitas, Tittle, Starr, Namath, Tarkenton, Jurgensen, and Staubach might never have lit up scoreboards. Where Shaughnessy invented and Halas perfected, Luckman executed—flawlessly.

At Columbia University in 1938, Luckman made the cover of *Life* magazine, with the headline, "Best Passer." That's exactly what Halas saw, so he traded two players and a draft choice to Pittsburgh to acquire Luckman. Then he offered Luckman the highest salary ever paid by the team at the time: $5,000 a year.

The money was not just for Luckman's throwing skills. Halas believed Luckman

At Columbia University in 1938, Luckman made the cover of Life *magazine, with the headline, "Best Passer."*

could run a hybrid offense in which the quarterback, not the runners or receivers, was the focal point. From his upright position a step behind the center, Luckman could "read" defensive alignments and make adjustments. He could change plays at the line of scrimmage, put men in motion. He could control the game.

Which is exactly what he did, turning quarterback into the NFL's glamour position, a notion that has not changed even as football heads into the 21st century.

Luckman was voted the NFL's MVP three times during his 12 seasons as a pro, and was selected All-Pro seven times. When he retired in 1950, his salary of $23,000 was matched only by Baugh's.

Oddly, it was during the 1940 NFL Championship game against Baugh and the Redskins that the T-formation took root. While the opposition was having a dismal day, the Bears won 73-0, scoring 11 touchdowns, helping popularize the offensive scheme, and beginning the demise of the traditional single wing.

Everyone saw the judiciousness of the T.

"Two years later," Baugh said, "we played the same bunch of boys, the same damn lineup. ... and we beat them."

The T-formation was here to stay. So was the NFL.

ARNIE, JACK AND TIGER

Arnold Palmer, Jack Nicklaus, and Tiger Woods

Although golf had many idols through the years—[Bobby] Jones, Walter Hagen, Sam Snead, Ben Hogan—none was a trailblazer. That chore was left to Palmer, who would perform it with élan.

Arnold Palmer won four Masters. Jack Nicklaus did him two better. The masters of golf for the last four decades agree that Tiger Woods could tame Augusta National as often as both of them combined.

"You can probably take Arnold's Masters and my Masters, add them together, and this kid should win more than that," Nicklaus said. "This kid is absolutely the most fundamentally sound golfer that I've seen at almost any age."

That's quite an assessment from the man generally regarded as the greatest of all golfers. Even if "this kid" wins half as often as Nicklaus or Palmer, he will be a special player.

And if Woods can duplicate what Palmer and Nicklaus did for the sport itself …

Palmer, the dominant golfer of the late 1950s and early 1960s, popularized a formerly elite sport. He brought it to the masses with a swashbuckling style that attracted blue-collar fans by the platoons: Arnie's Army, the near-rabid following that would routinely trek 18 holes of every round along with their links hero.

Nicklaus, chunky and even a bit clunky, knocked Palmer off the golf summit with a power game that Bobby Jones—American golf's first superstar, in the 1920s—once said was "a game with which I am not familiar."

But Nicklaus, thanks to overwhelming skills, a warm smile and, yes, a diet that took him from fat to fashionable, would have a huge impact on the sport, too. He would prove that athletes could compete at a high level while becoming powerful businessmen. "The Golden Bear" would be the first player to build a business empire while still in his prime.

Woods? Although his legacy is far from established, golf has experienced an unprecedented surge among minorities and youngsters since Woods turned pro in 1996 and turned the golfing world upside down.

None of what Nicklaus and Woods have achieved—or what Nancy Lopez did to popularize the women's tour in the 1970s— would have happened without Palmer. Although golf had many idols through the years—Jones, Walter Hagen, Sam Snead, Ben Hogan—none was a trailblazer. That chore was left to Palmer, who would perform it with élan.

"He was Every-man with a golf club in his hand," sportscaster Jack Whitaker said.

"It's not just what Arnold meant to golf," Lopez said. "It's what he meant to the whole country. He took the game to everyone."

Palmer was born September 10, 1929, in Latrobe, Pennsylvania, the son of a greenskeeper who later became the club pro at Latrobe Country Club. But for much of the 1930s, in tough times, he and his father hunted for rabbits and quail around the course.

Arnold owned his first set of clubs—sawed-off, naturally—at age three. Four years later, he was shooting around 100. By the time he was 12, Palmer could break 80.

After attending Wake Forest University and then spending three years in the Coast Guard, Palmer won the U.S. Amateur in 1954, which he said "gave me the confidence I needed to go play professional golf."

Hitching his pants as he prepared for a shot, smoking cigarettes in between strokes, scanning the crowd—often winking at fans—while his playing partners hit, Palmer's popularity soared as a pro. Nothing like the automatons who populated golf for decades, he'd spend time talking with the gallery. He'd grimace over bad shots, rejoice over good ones. His quick, slashing, non-classic swing endeared him to the people even more.

"He was Everyman with a golf club in his hand," sportscaster Jack Whitaker said. "The people in the galleries could see themselves in Arnold."

Of course, Palmer had to be successful on the links to inspire so much interest in golf. He won four Masters, two British Opens and a U.S. Open. More often than not, he made sensational fourth-round charges to win 60 times on the PGA Tour.

It was not until his first Masters win in 1958 that Arnie's Army took root. When it did, golf was changed forever.

"Arnold was the lightning rod for golf," said Frank Chirkinian, who produced the Masters for CBS for more than three decades. "His charm and his fire, combined with the ability of television to show the beauty of a place like Augusta, brought golf to a new level of popularity."

His style certainly endeared Palmer to television. He was Zorro, Hopalong Cassady, and Flash Gordon rolled into one, a made-for-TV hero. CBS, NBC, and ABC quickly discovered how marketable Palmer was. Live golf became a weekend staple of sports programming. Taped shows such as "Shell's Wonderful World of Golf," which included a Palmer-Nicklaus match among its 92 programs staged in 58 countries, sprouted everywhere.

Palmer became an icon in Europe and Asia, too. With the exception of Pele, no athlete of his era meant more to his sport or the people who followed it.

Just after his retirement from the NBA, golf fanatic Michael Jordan played a round with Palmer. "It's always a treat to play with him," Jordan said. "If you ever try to pattern your career after someone, look at Arnold. I have a lot of respect for him. It didn't take much for him to get me down here."

Arnold wasn't through when age took away his putting touch and some of the distance from his shots. He was instrumental in the development of the Senior Tour, and, naturally, was its first superstar.

"I wasn't very happy with how I was playing as I approached 50, but the idea of the Senior Tour was not that appealing, either," Palmer said. "I think there is

His style certainly endeared Palmer to television. He was Zorro, Hopalong Cassady and Flash Gordon rolled into one, a made-for-TV hero.

something in our makeup that drives us to want to stay where the elite are, and where the elite players are is the PGA Tour.

"But now, I believe it is one of the most important things I've been involved with, the Senior Tour. I think it was the most successful sports story of the decade [1980s]."

It was during that decade, in 1986, that Jack Nicklaus had his greatest triumph. At the age of 46, he won a sixth Masters, in the most dramatic fashion: a final-round blitz that carried him from far back in the pack to his final major title.

By then, Nicklaus had long ago overcome the scorn directed at him by Palmer's legions. Dubbed "Fat Jack," he stormed out of Ohio State and the amateur ranks to make his first professional victory a stunner—the 1962 U.S. Open at Oakmont Country Club in Palmer's backyard of western Pennsylvania. Nicklaus, whose length off the tee and precise putting stroke made him a factor for more than three decades, won an 18-hole playoff with Palmer by three strokes, despite the loud preferences expressed by the fans.

At 22, Nicklaus had fashioned a changing of the guard in golf. "I think Jack and I were great for each other, on the course and off," Palmer said.

On the course, Nicklaus would eclipse everyone. He would win 20 majors, capped by the '86 Masters at an age when most golfers are has-beens on the regular tour. He would continue to contend in the biggest tournaments well into his

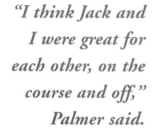

"I think Jack and I were great for each other, on the course and off," Palmer said.

fifties, and after losing weight without sacrificing any of the power or precision of his game, Nicklaus also would become a superstar. Events such as the Skins Game—a four-man, made-for-television, 18-hole get-together marked by a jovial camaraderie mixed with intense competitiveness—would draw strong television ratings thanks to the presence of Jack. And Arnie.

Off the course, Nicklaus would become a dominating player, too. Although there were setbacks involving non-golf businesses, his sports empire made the Golden Bear golden. Now considered the foremost course designer among star players, Nicklaus is so in demand that, several years ago, he estimated the waiting time for new projects at three years. He bought MacGregor Golf and turned it into a force in a highly competitive, technological, and costly business. In the year after Nicklaus took a more active role in his companies in 1985, revenue doubled. And his involvement certainly did not hurt his golf game, which was sharp enough for him to win another Masters, then turn to the Senior Tour and continue to win consistently.

In the '90s, health problems plagued both Palmer and Nicklaus. Arnie successfully overcame prostate cancer, while Jack needed a hip replacement. Both quickly recovered and returned to the one place they felt most comfortable: the golf course. Usually, neither of them turned out to be much of a threat. But the fans didn't mind.

Now considered the foremost course designer among star players, Nicklaus is so in demand that, several years ago, he estimated the waiting time for new projects at three years.

"It seems no matter how we're playing, [the fans] are there, and that is wonderful for Arnold and myself," Nicklaus said. "Of course, I'd like to reward their loyalty with a few more birdies."

"It seems no matter how we're playing, [the fans] are there, and that is wonderful for Arnold and myself," Nicklaus said. "Of course, I'd like to reward their loyalty with a few more birdies."

But at the turn of the century, the low scores and big paydays belong to the youngsters. And none of those youngsters has had the impact of Eldrick "Tiger" Woods.

Already seen putting on TV shows like "That's Incredible" and "The Mike Douglas Show" by the time he was five, Woods was reared by his father, Earl, and mother, Tida, to be a pro golfer. And not just any pro golfer, but the leader of the sport, the catalyst for the influx of minority players into the game.

Woods is proud of his heritage—Earl is black, Tida is Thai—and the role he has played in the rapid popularization of golf, particularly among lower-income and minority players. But he doesn't shy away from the view that his first responsibility is winning tournaments, not being a cultural and social reformer.

"When I look around and see all of the kids who are taking up the game and the makeup of my galleries, it's great," he said. "If they respond to me and take an interest in golf, of course I'm all for that.

"But my obligation is to my game. Playing golf is my profession."

Not since Nicklaus has an amateur come onto the PGA Tour with the kind of credentials or fan-following that Woods brought in 1996. He won an impressive three straight U.S. Junior championships and followed with an even more astounding feat: three successive U.S. Amateur crowns. He was a star player at Stanford University before cutting short his college stay to turn pro—and sign a $40 million endorsement deal with Nike.

Two months after joining the tour, competing against the best players in the world, Woods won the Las Vegas Invitational. A few weeks later, he won again, at the Walt Disney World Classic. The kid earned his tour card in just seven events, winning two of them.

Like Palmer and Nicklaus, Woods was winning on the fairways and greens. His powerhouse swing and the length it produced were mesmerizing. Golf officials actually began discussing redesigns on some courses that would become too short—obsolete—in the face of such prodigious shots.

And he was winning away from the arena.

Nike's advertising campaign, "I Am Tiger Woods," brilliantly played off the twenty-something Woods' attractiveness to youngsters. Within weeks of his early success on tour, sporting goods stores and equipment outlets were heavily stocked with the Woods brand. Almost immediately, those brands began selling; much of the merchandise was purchased by golfing neophytes.

"In my estimation, it opens a lot of doors," Woods said of his popularity, "and draws lot of people into golf who never thought of playing the game."

Woods' journey to South Africa in 1998—like the first tour by a black cricket team from the West Indies and the appointment of a black man to head the rugby league there—was a morale boost for the majority of the nation's people in the days after the fall of apartheid.

"He's the one great black golfer we have seen," said Soweto Golf Club president Mike Nompula. "He has made it."

Woods' emergence also had a profound effect on golf's relationship with television. The PGA, riding the wave of Tigermania, negotiated a mammoth new deal that began in 1999. The four-year package with six networks included regular tour events in prime time, the addition of three World Championship Series events, and coverage of the first and second rounds at every tournament. By 2002, the PGA should take in close to $200 million in television money, while significantly increasing the number of programming hours.

PGA Tour commissioner Tim Finchem recognized Woods' role in the process. "Any player who will move the needle on the ratings like he does, has significant topspin on the negotiations," Finchem said.

But to undisputably establish himself among the greats, Woods needed to win a major. He came to the 1997 Masters as one of the favorites, and what Tiger achieved surpassed anything Arnie or Jack ever managed. Or perhaps envisioned.

After shooting a 40 on his first nine, a score that would have led to missing the cut by miles if he didn't improve, Woods went wild. On the perfect course for him, long and wide, Woods became relentless. Birdies and eagles seemed to drop out of the dogwoods and azaleas right onto his scorecard.

Following the third round, when he held an unheard-of nine-stroke lead, Woods allowed himself to peek ahead and examine what it would mean for a black man to wear the green jacket. "I think [that] on this kind of stage, with this kind of media," he said, "it would do a lot for the game as far as minority golf is concerned."

"[At the 1997 Masters] birdies and eagles seemed to drop out of the dogwoods and azaleas right onto his scorecard."

"When I look around and see all the kids who are taking up the game, and the makeup of my galleries, it's great..."

His victory the next day, by a whopping 12 strokes, before a record television audience, did something for all of golf. It established Woods as the successor to Palmer and Nicklaus. And it showed just how unbeatable an upper-echelon athlete at the peak of his game can be.

"You envision dueling it out with Faldo, or Nicklaus or Watson, someone who is always tough to beat down the stretch, or birdieing 16, 17 and 18 to get into a playoff," Woods said. "But never in the fashion I did. That's something you never dream of. It's kind of nice that it became a reality."

And Tiger is just getting started.

The authors wish to acknowledge the following research sources for

THEY CHANGED THE GAME

American Heritage	The Reader's Companion to American History
American History	The Saturday Evening Post
The Associated Press Archives	Smithsonian Magazine
Auto Racing Digest	Soccer Digest
Canadian Press	Sport
Current Biography Yearbook	Sport Business
Daytona USA archives	Sports Illustrated
Esquire Magazine	Sports Illustrated for Kids
Football Digest	Tennis Magazine
Football News	The Record of Bergen County
Forbes	The Ring Magazine
Golf Digest	The Rockland Journal-News
Golf Magazine	The Sporting News
Golf World	Time
Jet	Track and Field News
Los Angeles Times	USA Today
National Football League archives	USA Weekend
New York Daily News	U.S. Olympic Committee archives
New York Times	Wall Street Journal
Newsday	Washington Post
Newsweek	Washington Times
Olympian Magazine	Women's Sports and Fitness
Philadelphia Daily News	

Photo Credits

Allsport Photography—vi, 4, 5, 10, 13, 23, 24, 26, 27, 34, 35, 36, 37, 38, 39, 40, 41, 42, 43, 44, 46, 52, 53, 54, 55, 56, 59, 60, 61, 62, 66, 67, 68, 69, 73, 79, 80, 89, 90, 93, 105, 118, 119, 121, 123, 126, 129, 130, 143, 144, 145, 146, 147, 148, 149, 150, 151, 152,

AP Wide World Photos—6, 7, 8, 9, 11, 12, 14, 15, 17, 18, 22, 28, 29, 31, 32, 33, 47, 48, 49, 51, 58, 63, 64, 65, 72, 74, 75, 78, 81, 82, 83, 84, 85, 86, 87, 88, 91, 92, 94, 95, 96, 97, 98, 99, 100, 102, 109, 111, 112, 113, 114, 115, 120, 122, 128, 131, 133, 136, 140, 141, 142

Corbis/Bettman—16, 20, 70, 104, 106, 107, 108, 116, 117, 124, 125, 127 135, 139

London Life-Portnay/HHOF—76

Fred Keenan/HHOF—77